Facilitating Organizational Change

ASTD LEARNING SYSTEM

Module 5

ASTD PRESS

ASTD Press is an internationally renowned source of insightful and practical information on workplace learning and performance topics, including training basics, evaluation and return-on-investment (ROI), instructional systems development (ISD), e-learning, leadership, and career development.

Ordering information: The *ASTD Learning System* and other books published by ASTD Press can be purchased by visiting our website at http://store.astd.org or by calling 800.628.2783 or 703.683.8100.

Library of Congress Control Number: 2006920960

ISBN-10: 1-56286-443-2

ISBN-13: 978-1-56286-443-9

ASTD Press Staff
Director: Anthony Allen
Manager, Acquisitions and Author Relations: Justin Brusino
Editorial Manager: Larry Fox
Sr. Associate Editor: Tora Estep
Associate Editor: Ashley McDonald
Editorial Assistant: Stephanie Castellano
Production Coordinator: Glenn Saltzman
Cover Design: Alizah Epstein

Composition by Stephen McDougal, Mechanicsville, Maryland, www.alphawebtech.net

Contents

1. **Systems Thinking and Open Systems Theory**. 1

   What Is Systems Thinking? 2
   What Is Open Systems Theory? 5

2. **Chaos and Complexity Theory** 13

   Chaos and Complexity Theory Defined 14
   How Chaos and Complexity Relate to Change 14
   Similarities and Differences Between Chaos and Complexity 20
   OD Intervention 21

3. **Appreciative Inquiry Theory** 27

   Background. 28
   Leading Groups or Teams 29
   Effective Questioning Techniques 30
   Multidisciplinary Learning Topics 35
   Experiential Activities to Expand Learning 36
   Organizational Realignment 40

4. **Action Learning** 47

   Six Components of Action Learning 48
   Action Learning and Learning Organizations 49
   Bloom's Taxonomy 50
   Six Sigma Processes 50
   Kepner-Tregoe Process. 51
   Action Learning Groups 52
   Meeting Management 57
   Multicultural (Global) Groups 61

5. **Systems, Culture, and Leadership in an Organizational System** 67

   Leadership Within an Organizational Context 68
   Defining Leadership 68
   Evolution of Organizational Structures 70
   Evolution of Leadership Models 76
   Comparing Leadership to Management 81
   Leadership Styles 82
   Forces of Change on Organizations. 83
   The Need for a Learning Culture. 87
   Defining a Learning Culture 88
   Role of WLP Professionals in Leading Change 90

6. **Change Theory and Change Models** **99**

Defining the Current State 100

Defining Intended Outcomes 100

Selling the Change Strategy 101

Planning for Change 102

Analyzing Stakeholders 104

Cultural Implications 105

Milestone Evaluations 105

Introducing Change 106

Overcoming Resistance 107

Reactions to Change 108

Implementing Change 109

Evaluating Effects of Change 111

7. **Process Thinking and Design** **117**

8. **Engagement Practices** **119**

Needs Analysis for Change 120

Six Sigma Practices for Change 120

Communicating Issues to the Workforce 121

Owning the Process 123

9. **Communication Theory** **127**

Communication and Facilitating Change 128

Communication Styles 132

Communication Channels 138

10. **Diversity and Inclusion** **145**

11. **Motivation Theory** **147**

Motivation Best Practices 148

Employee Motivators 148

Motivating Learners 155

12. **Mindset and Mental Models** **163**

Management Styles 164

Personal Social Styles 164

Emotional Intelligence 165

13. **Appendix A: Glossary** **169**

14. **Appendix B: Answer Key** **173**

15. **Appendix C: Index** **187**

Introduction

Managing change in organizations continually grows in **complexity** as the workplace continues to redefine itself. Today's workplace learning and performance (WLP) professionals will face change in almost every aspect of their careers, as well as assume a number of roles when facilitating change. Those roles can include change agent, leader, facilitator, sponsor, coach—and, ultimately, a champion of the change strategy. From establishing ownership of the initiative to modeling change themselves, WLP professionals will be called upon to plan, assess, implement, support, and evaluate all phases of the change process.

There are numerous theories and approaches that relate to organizational change, including **systems thinking**, appreciative inquiry, **chaos** and complexity, and **action research**. Because the purpose of the *ASTD Learning System* is to help you become familiar with the theory behind the application, this module will explore those theories relative to change as they apply to the body of knowledge in the ASTD Competency Model.

The authors of the *ASTD Competency Study** defined a set of key knowledge related to each area of expertise (AOE) that were used to form the chapters of the *ASTD Learning System*. Among the chapters of this module, there are two that relate to, or cross over with, other modules. Chapter 7, "Process Thinking and Design," refers to chapter 5 of Module 8: *Managing Organizational Knowledge*, and chapter 10, "Diversity and Inclusion," refers to chapter 12 in Module 9: *Career Planning and Talent Management*. These crossover chapters provide additional information that is specific to the given AOE, but is discussed in detail elsewhere in the *ASTD Learning System*.

The amount of effort required to successfully manage change is too numerous to list here, but the authors of the study defined a set of key actions that provide some essential behaviors and activities required for facilitating change. Along with these actions come concrete examples of work, or outputs—the tangible items that the professional creates. The following table provides some examples of key actions and outputs related to facilitating change.

Key Actions (Do)	Examples of Outputs (Deliver)
• Establish sponsorship and ownership for change	• Strategy for involving stakeholders and engaging employees
• Conduct diagnostic assessments • Provide feedback	• Change needs assessment • Case for change

Key Actions (Do)	Examples of Outputs (Deliver)
• Facilitate strategic planning for change • Create a contract for change	• Change strategy • Design requirements • Change plan, including outcomes, expectations, milestone events, and appropriate pacing • Metrics to measure change outcomes and change process
• Build involvement • Support the change intervention	• Communication strategy
• Integrate change into organizational culture • Model mastery of leading change	• New models of programs or approaches
• Manage consequences	• Documented contingency plans
• Evaluate change results	• Project reports • Evaluation report documenting effect of change and best practices

For further detailed information about the key knowledge, key actions, and outputs, refer to *ASTD Competency Study: Mapping the Future* (2004).*

*Bernthal, P.R., et al. (2004). *The ASTD Competency Study: Mapping the Future*. Alexandria, VA: ASTD Press.

1
Systems Thinking and Open Systems Theory

Approaching organizational change requires an understanding of systems. All processes, even those that have little organization structure, can be examined provided the workplace learning and performance (WLP) professional uses appropriate systems thinking. How the system affects the process and where a systematic solution may be offered are central to facilitating organizational change.

Every organization strives for continuous improvement. Systems thinking offers one opportunity for accomplishing this task. To begin, systems thinking must be positioned as one of the key disciplines of organizational learning. In fact, it has often been referred to as the cornerstone discipline. According to author Peter Senge (1994), organizational learning is a process within organizations in which people at all levels, individually and collectively, are continually increasing their capacity to learn and produce results they really care about.

Learning Objectives:

- ☑ Describe the importance of applying systems thinking theory to change initiatives.

- ☑ List the benefits, characteristics, and perspectives of systems thinking.

- ☑ Explain how *open systems theory* applies to facilitating change.

What Is Systems Thinking?

Systems thinking looks at a problem from a holistic perspective. It puts a problem into a context of the larger whole with the objective of finding the most effective place to make an appropriate ***intervention***. Systems thinking involves determining what underlying, fundamental relationships are causing the problem to avoid being forced to react and continually put out fires. Systems thinking allows for recognition and work with any series of small changes, adapting and making plans that will benefit the organization—before the situation reaches a crisis stage.

Systems thinking encompasses looking at all of the ramifications of all decisions and strategies. It questions the types of behaviors that are being rewarded, and, if the firefighting kind of reaction is being rewarded, what would happen in the organization if people started to be rewarded for making long-term, systematic changes. Systems thinking is a method of deep thinking that involves a shift in perspective to the whole of an organization and, in that process, enables people to pause and reflect on what is really important. This way, actions that are undertaken are more imaginative, creative, and effective.

Benefits of Systems Thinking

Employing systems thinking means being better able to understand the ramifications of decisions. The organization will be able to assess a situation and determine where to make the most effective intervention. These benefits have been attributed to using systems thinking:

- more knowledge (the right questions asked)
- stakeholder involvement in the process
- a shared understanding of the problem
- many perspectives considered and integrated
- a vision beyond day-to-day events
- a long-term view by key decision makers
- the big picture seen as a competitive advantage.

Characteristics of Systems Thinking

When organizations start to think systemically, they will notice that the way they look at any problem begins to change. Of course, these changes take time and are part of a gradual process, but they do encompass a transformation in the thinking process. This change will have long-lasting and beneficial effects, both professionally and personally for employees. A systems thinker will be able to

- understand complex relationships and interdependencies
- take responsibility to fix the problem

- balance short-term and long-term needs and perspectives
- reframe an issue or problem
- see the entirety of a situation
- discern patterns of recurring problems not driven by daily events
- question any and all underlying assumptions
- develop understanding and compassion.

Principles of Systems Thinking

The following basic principles of systems thinking are based on Draper L. Kauffman's book *Systems 1: An Introduction to Systems Thinking* (1980) and Peter Senge's *The Fifth Discipline Fieldbook* (1994).

There Are No Final or Right Answers

When dealing with a complex system and its many interdependencies, WLP professionals look for the best place to make a change—the place that will have the most leverage in helping to solve the problem.

Cause and Effect Are Not Related to Time and Space

When looking for the most leverage to solve the problem, it is important to first look back over time to find the root cause. The leverage to solve the problem will rarely be found near the symptoms of the problem.

Solutions Require Careful Consideration

There will be time delays with any solutions proposed. These delays need to be considered when making a decision. For example, the staff is becoming burned out because they have been working a lot of overtime hours. The organization decides to hire a consultant to deliver training to the staff on how to manage this stress. The amount of time it takes to acquire the training and then implement the stress reduction strategies is a factor to consider when creating a plan.

Behavior Gets Worse Before It Gets Better

Through the process of modifying a system, there will be some resistance to the change. Behavior may go from bad to worse during this transition. As members of the group begin to see the benefits of the shift in thinking, new patterns of behavior start to emerge.

There Are Limits in Every System

Nothing can grow forever. Eventually, limits will be reached and an awareness of these limits to growth is an essential first step in learning how to manage a system.

Foresight Benefits the Organization

Solutions to problems affecting **complex systems** usually take some time to resolve. Waiting until a problem suddenly develops and then being forced to react to the situation does not leave enough time to determine the best possible solution. If, however, resources are allocated toward a plan that anticipates potential problems, more choices will be available to make the kind of decision that is valuable to the organization.

In the Real World: Healthcare Field

In *Best Practices in Knowledge Management and Organizational Learning Handbook* (2000), John Couris, senior manager of quality management and education at Massachusetts General Hospital, writes that the radiology and the orthopedic departments of that hospital independently decided to study the service they provide their patients. Initially, each organization vertically focused its service improvement activities in an attempt to incrementally enhance the patient experience from a departmental perspective.

With the advent of new technology and a web-image distribution system, both departments began to look horizontally at services provided to patients, using a systems thinking approach. They understood that looking at the care process as a system was essential to the long-term success of both departments as they strove to provide the best patient care. Neither department could afford to continue to look at its processes as simply functional or linear operations. Doing so was too costly in terms of duplication of effort and financial outlay and had a negative effect on operating efficiencies.

Implementation faced some challenges: achieving total buy-in from leaders of the departments, navigation of the political landscape of both organizations, and allocation of resources. To address these challenges, the departments created an Orthopedic-Radiology Committee (now called the Computed Radiography Committee). In addition, they implemented a leadership training series that focused on systems thinking.

Ultimately, these two groups understood the importance of looking at the operations as one system. The benefits realized by leveraging technology and systems thinking included reducing patient throughput time by 34 percent and setting the stage for the proliferation of systems thinking as a leadership and management tool with the radiology and orthopedics departments.

Perspectives of Systems Thinking

Three trainers quit last Friday. What could happen in this situation? Most people have the tendency to react in a similar way to such events: panic. However, by stepping back for a moment and trying to see the bigger picture that may be causing this particular situation, it is possible to have a much better understanding of the hows and whys of

Figure 1-1. Levels of Problems

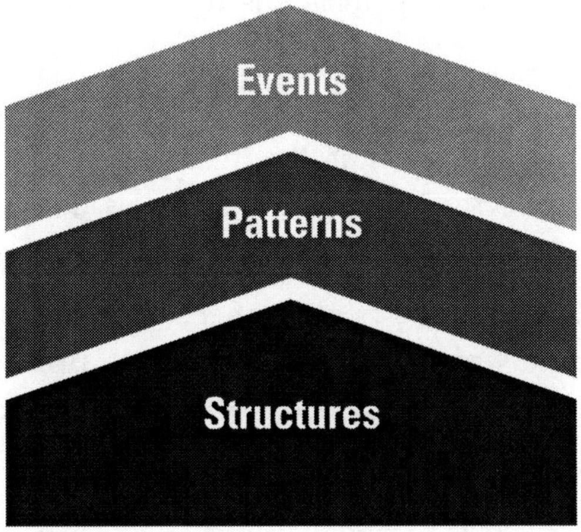

Source: Kim (1994).

the event. Figure 1-1 depicts the three ways or perspectives to view a problem.

The situation just described illustrates the events level: *Something* happened, and the first response is to simply react to that *something*. The next level, patterns, goes a step deeper into the problem. By having determined how many times something has happened, the process of seeing a pattern develop begins. Viewing a problem from the structures level enables practitioners to ask questions, such as, "What underlying structures are producing patterns of behavior that we are seeing with this problem?" In other words, what is or are the underlying root cause(s) of the problem at hand?

When deciding to take an action, it is important to ask what ramifications that action will have in an organization, both above and below the level at which the decision was made. Management policies and decisions can create confusion and can unwittingly be the source of a faltering system. Dealing with elements at the level of the underlying structure increases the leverage toward finding workable solutions to the organization's problems.

What Is Open Systems Theory?

Open systems theory is the view that any organization is a system that absorbs such environmental inputs as people factors, raw materials, capital, and information; uses them in such transformational processes as service delivery or manufacturing methods; and expels them as outputs such as finished goods or customer services. Regardless of an organization's function and size, it is a complex system made up of internal and external related and interdependent pieces. By examining both the internal and external parts and how they interrelate, it is possible to gain a greater understanding of what influences affect or are affected by the organization.

Open systems theory is an important starting point for thinking about performance. An open system is characterized by inputs (such as people, capital, or information) that processes (such as work methods or procedures) transform into outputs (such as products or services). All open systems draw resources from an external environment (or suprasystem), receive feedback about how well outputs were received, and derive benefits from interactions with the external environment. Benefits may include profits, high ***return-on-investment (ROI)***, or customer satisfaction. Subsystems are parts of organizations that contribute to the success of the system within the suprasystem.

Organizations use open systems to create products and services. They pull raw material, information, capital, and people as inputs from the external environment. Work processes apply value-adding activities to the inputs. Organizations expel the resulting work-process outputs into the environment.

Performance is the result of an effective interaction among the resources, process, people, and environment. An organization's performance is efficient if the organization is doing things right. An organization's performance is effective if the organization is doing the right things.

Taking action on any aspect of the system may improve performance. If an organization can increase the quantity or quality of inputs so that they better match up to the organization's needs at the beginning of the work processes, performance may improve. Similarly, if an organization can increase the quantity or quality of processes so that they better match up to desired outputs, performance may improve. Performance may also improve if the quantity or quality of outputs increases to better match up to what customers in the external environment desire, or if the organization increases the quality or quantity of information received from the environment to anticipate future changes in the suprasystem (which planners often do during the strategic planning process).

Systems View

Regardless of the tools used to collect information and data about an organization, taking a systems view is imperative. A systems view recognizes the interrelationships of the parts and the importance of their interaction to create the whole. This view is sometimes difficult because individuals exist within the system, and it is hard to stand outside to see the whole. These questions can help maintain a systems perspective:

- Are department and unit strategies linked to the organization-wide strategy?

- Who are the department's internal and external customers?

- What are the department's products and services?

- What are the customer's requirements for those products and services?

- Is performance measured on the basis of how well those products and services meet customers' requirements?

- Who are the department's internal and external suppliers?

- Are clear goals established for the products and services provided by the suppliers?

- Is there documentation for the department's role in the cross-functional processes?

- Is the department measured according to the degree to which it contributes to cross-functional processes?

- Is the upstream performance of the processes that flow through the department measured?

- Are there tracking and feedback systems that effectively and efficiently gather performance information and provide it to the people who need it?

- Does the client have the skills to troubleshoot (remove the root causes of) performance gaps in the system?

- Does the client spend a large percentage of time working to improve the interfaces between the department and other functions and among the subunits within the department?

- Do employees work in an environment where job design, goals, feedback, rewards, resources, and training enable them to make maximum contributions to process efficiency and effectiveness?

The ability to stand at the edge, to see the patterns, connections, and underlying structures that create the dynamics of a situation is one of the most significant organizational contributions. However, it is difficult to be a member of a system. A WLP professional must analyze the parts based on the assumption that if organizational members understand the individual parts, they will master the whole. Simply focusing on events as a series of parts limits the possibilities to a reactive stance. Look for patterns of behavior and the underlying structures that generate those patterns.

The new, scientific approach teaches that organizations are fluid, interdependent, and constantly changing. To harness the positive energy in the system, the organization must be recognized as a living system. The value is to make visible the connections and interrelationships beneath the surface of a series of events. Only by discovering the structural underpinnings for behavioral patterns can organizational or performance change be implemented.

✓ Chapter 1 Knowledge Check

1. **Employing systems thinking allows an organization to assess a situation holistically and determine where to make the most effective intervention.**

    __ **A.** True

    __ **B.** False

2. **The management team of a manufacturing firm is constantly reacting to new problems and does not seem to have the time to make long-range plans. The management team needs to apply a systems thinking approach because**

    __ **A.** It will help identify the most appropriate training solutions needed to fix the problems

    __ **B.** It will help identify the employees who are best at resolving crises

    __ **C.** It will allow the management team to uncover the root causes contributing to the problems and consider the effect of any implemented changes

    __ **D.** The organization will not thrive without long-range planning

3. **Which of the following recognizes the interrelationships of the parts and the importance of their interaction to create the whole?**

    __ **A.** Systems thinking

    __ **B.** Systems view

    __ **C.** Open systems theory

    __ **D.** Fifth discipline theory

4. **One of the benefits of systems thinking is the ability to discern patterns of recurring problems not driven by daily events.**

    __ **A.** True

    __ **B.** False

5. **Which of the following is *not* one of the three perspectives on problems?**

    __ **A.** Events

    __ **B.** Patterns

    __ **C.** Resources

    __ **D.** Structures

6. **Which of the following is *not* a characteristic of a systems thinker?**

___ **A.** Takes responsibility to fix the problem

___ **B.** Focuses on independent, mutually exclusive relationships

___ **C.** Discerns patterns of recurring problems not driven by daily events

___ **D.** Balances short-term and long-term needs and perspectives

7. **Which of the following is *not* a principle of systems thinking?**

___ **A.** Solutions should be decided and implemented as quickly as possible.

___ **B.** Cause and effect are not related to time and space.

___ **C.** There are no final or right answers.

___ **D.** Behavior gets worse before it gets better.

8. **The chief learning officer (CLO) of a consulting firm needs to recruit a training director with strong systems thinking capabilities. In preparation for the interview, the CLO is compiling a list of needed skills. In reviewing the candidates' references, one candidate's description should eliminate this candidate from the pool because this characteristic is not indicative of a systems thinker. Which candidate should be eliminated?**

___ **A.** Candidate A. In making decisions demonstrates an understanding of complex relationships and interdependencies

___ **B.** Candidate B. In making decisions responds quickly and decisively to unforeseen events as they arise

___ **C.** Candidate C. In making decisions always balances short-term and long-term needs and perspectives

___ **D.** Candidate D. In making decisions always questions the underlying assumptions

9. **Which of the following theories postulates the view that any organization is a system that absorbs such environmental inputs as people factors, raw materials, capital, and information; uses them in such transformational processes as service delivery or manufacturing methods; and expels them as outputs, such as finished goods or customer services?**

___ **A.** Systems thinking

___ **B.** Systems view

___ **C.** Open systems theory

___ **D.** Fifth discipline theory

10. Open systems theory examines

    A. Inputs/outputs and external/internal relationships

    B. Closed versus open organizations

    C. Events, patterns, and structures

    D. All software used to manage the enterprise

References

Albrecht, K. (1983). *Organization Development: A Total Systems Approach to Positive Change in Any American Organization.* Upper Saddle River, NJ: Prentice Hall.

Couris, J., C. Zulauf, and C. Kennedy. (2000). *Best Practices in Knowledge Management and Organizational Learning Handbook.* Burlington, MA: Linkage.

Kauffman, D.L. (1980). *Systems 1: An Introduction to Systems Thinking.* Minneapolis: Future Systems.

Kim, D.H. (1994). *Systems Archetypes: Toolbox Reprint Series.* Cambridge, MA: Pegasus Communications.

Rothwell, W.J., et al. (1999). *ASTD Models for Workplace Learning and Performance: Roles, Competencies, and Outputs.* Alexandria, VA: ASTD Press.

Scott, B. (2000). *Consulting on the Inside.* Alexandria, VA: ASTD Press.

Senge, P.M. (1994). *The Fifth Discipline Fieldbook: Strategies and Tools for Building a Learning Organization.* New York: Currency/Doubleday.

Zulauf, C.A. (1997). "Systems Thinking." *Infoline* No. 259703.

2
Chaos and Complexity Theory

Chaos theory is based on an underlying assumption that order exists even though it is not immediately identifiable. Complexity theory considers chaos as one mode of behavior within the theory. Using both theories to approach each organizational change initiative offers the workplace learning and performance (WLP) professional a view of uncertainty.

Traditionally, managers learn that the right way of supervising employees involves careful planning, coordination, and control. In reality, however, management behavior is often unplanned, random, and contingent. In today's fast-changing and competitive work environment, plans often derail and managers have less time to coordinate and control the actions of their employees.

This chapter defines the ***chaos and complexity theory*** and applies this theory to business management. By describing the characteristics of the chaos and complexity theory found in organizations, this chapter presents guidelines for applying the chaos and complexity theory to an organization. Additionally, the chapter addresses the pros and cons of applying this theory, discusses how it relates to organizational change, and describes the implications on trainers and ***organization development (OD)*** interventions.

Learning Objectives:

- ☑ Define the concepts behind the chaos and complexity theory.
- ☑ Identify how the chaos and complexity theory relates to organizational change.
- ☑ Describe the similarities and differences between chaos and complexity.
- ☑ Describe how chaos and complexity apply to developing a change solution.

Chaos and Complexity Theory Defined

More than 30 years ago, the chaos and complexity theory began to take shape in the scientific world. A critical leap occurred in 1977 at the University of California, Santa Cruz, when a group of doctoral students began exploring the ways in which order emerges from chaos. Borrowing theories that physicists and mathematicians had been exploring for decades, they discovered that the universe is a vibrant and chaotic system, not a static machine subject to our control. As their research progressed, the students determined that, although the universe and other systems are extremely complex, they contain patterns that can lead to a greater understanding of their structures and an ability to predict patterns that they will follow.

Just what are chaos and complexity anyway? Answers vary depending on the person providing the definition. Purists would criticize combining the terms because they represent distinct theories from different disciplines. Some explain the difference between the two by saying chaos is the study of how simple systems can generate complicated behavior, whereas complexity is the study of how complicated systems generate simple behavior.

How Chaos and Complexity Relate to Change

How does chaos and complexity theory translate into good organizational management? How and why would someone want to apply these scientific theories to business organizations? The reason is this: Since the introduction of the Aristotelian-Ptolemaic System (which first presented a controlled order for the planets), humans have attempted to find order in their environment.

Today, organizations continue this struggle for order in the way business organizations are managed. Many want to create organizational charts, place everyone in a box, and line up these boxes in a linear and hierarchical fashion. With the surge of this new science and knowledge that scientific theories historically progress into the science of business, organizations that apply the basic principles involved in the chaos and complexity theory can learn to exploit their environment and co-evolve with other chaotic organizations.

As research into the chaos and complexity theory has become more widespread, organizational experts have found that organizations are near perfect examples of complex, nonlinear dynamic systems—phenomena usually studied by theoretical physicists, mathematicians, and biologists.

Characteristics of Complex Systems

All complex systems share certain characteristics—it does not matter if they relate to the physical world or to organizations. Although theorists do not agree on which characteristics are most important, most accept the following as a central part of the chaos and complexity theory.

The Whole Is More Than the Parts

Traditionally, the best way to understand a complex system is to break it down into smaller, more manageable chunks. If a system is examined one component at a time, it's difficult to see how each component interacts with other components, much less see how everything works together. As a result, vital information is not readily apparent.

Patterns Appear Throughout the System

All complex systems are made up of a limited number of repeating patterns. Although they may appear to occur randomly, one can look closely and see that certain behaviors and qualities appear repeatedly. In business, common actions and attitudes in members echo on different levels and at different parts of an organization. Even when the system changes, these actions and attitudes stay within certain invisible boundaries.

Cause and Effect Is Never Simple

It can be difficult to determine whether one action caused another to occur. Most events in complex systems have multiple causes that are not always closely linked in time and space; thus, to isolate one action and examine it may give an inaccurate perception. For example, if fish are observed swerving in response to the approach of another fish, one might assume that the first fish was responding only to the approach of the other one. To pan back and look at the entire school, however, one would see that the first fish's actions were influenced by—and part of—a complex system in which each member of the school acts to keep the school together and moving in the same direction.

Inaccurate assumptions like this also occur in organizations. Work groups often have a problem person who is subtly or overtly blamed for conflicts and difficulties within the group. If this individual is observed interacting with only one or two other group members, one may come to the conclusion that the blame is well placed. When this problem person leaves the group, however, the problem often resurfaces in different ways—whether in the guise of another problem person or not. By ceasing observation of the individual and observing the group as a whole, it should be apparent why the group has a problem to begin with.

History Does and Doesn't Repeat Itself

Although patterns appear throughout systems, subtle differences emerge each time a pattern is repeated. Patterns may seem to be identical, but complex systems are aperiodic—they never repeat in exactly the same way. The same actions will never produce exactly the same results. For example, if a survey were given to the same group of people at various times, the responses would never be exactly the same. One could, however, predict the general pattern of the responses by analyzing past surveys given to that group.

Change Comes From Chaos

All systems constantly evolve. Some changes come smoothly; others are more disruptive. A system will resist change for as long as it can. Although the system attempts to resist the change by keeping its current form, this change will continue to build pressure upon the system. This increasing instability throws the system into chaotic imbalance. At this point, sudden dramatic change will occur because the system will either reinvent itself to meet new challenges or disintegrate under the strain.

Take a balloon, for example. Inflate it and the balloon expands to accommodate the added air. At a certain point, the added air places so much of a strain upon the balloon that it can no longer accommodate the increased volume, and it pops. Although this chaotic imbalance can be just as traumatic for organizations as it is for the balloon, the system usually finds a new level of stability after adapting to the changes.

The Future Can and Can't Be Predicted

When dealing with complex systems, the effect that an action will have on the entire system is never certain. Even the smallest differences get exaggerated over time—that is, small stones cast into the organizational pond can create huge ripples throughout the system. Although exact quantitative predictions are impossible, one can make relatively accurate guesses about the qualitative aspects of a system.

For example, when conducting a training program, one can be reasonably certain that everyone learned at least some of what the trainer was teaching. How much participants remember and how well they apply that information back on the job cannot be predicted.

Complexity Theory

The central premise of the complexity theory as it relates to organizations is that order can emerge out of chaos. The key for managers is to first develop a strong sense of vision in employees and then to step back and allow the employees to determine the detailed courses of action themselves. This vision should be strategic and contain a clear sense of the broader mission of the organization rather than stipulate specific paths. If employees are given the tools and freedom to chart their own paths, they will be able to choose the best course of action to reach the organization's goals. They will also be able to adapt to changing situations and improve processes as they discover new and better ways of doing their jobs.

Johan Roos (1997) states that organizations that master complexity theory succeed because they perform these tasks:

- Know their identity.

- Explore and exploit their environment.

- Interact and co-evolve with other organizations.

- Study a relationship among its component parts.

Using these tasks as group headings, Roos suggests that organizations pursue the following 10 strategies.

Identity

1. Recognize identity as the basis for the self-referencing essential to knowledge development.

2. Recognize that identity both provides tools to explore the possibilities for the organization and limits the organization's ability to see other paths.

3. Realize that the organization's identity can be shaped by external forces and will change accordingly. Resisting this change can damage the organization and lead to chaos.

Knowledge Development

4. Prioritize knowledge development, recognizing that the environment could change at any moment.

5. Reflect on external factors that could require new knowledge or cause the organization to alter its path.

6. Develop knowledge by recognizing patterns rather than by attempting to guess what the future holds.

Co-Evolution

7. Develop knowledge through relationships, including strategic alliances, mergers, and acquisitions.

8. Form alliances that have at least some degree of regularity, a combination of chaos and stability.

Internal Relationships

9. Recognize and interpret the relationships among internal parts or agents as well as their relationships to the environment as a whole.

10. Seek a level of interconnectedness among the organization's component parts that reflect its environment and goals. Too much interconnectedness can inhibit growth as much as too little.

Complexity in Organizations

By adhering to strategies such as those just listed, organizations show how chaos and complexity theory focuses attention on information and feedback mechanisms. These mechanisms bring information that is essential to forming strategies and relationships both within and outside the organization. In this way, it is quite similar to two accepted management practices: learning organizations and systems thinking.

The Learning Organization

Organizations that implement the chaos and complexity theory share many of the characteristics of learning organizations. To adapt quickly to changing circumstances and flock resources around projects, organizations need to create an environment in which constant learning is a major part of its culture. Learning organizations accept the fact that nothing is completely stable and that they must be prepared to quickly change their strategies to adapt.

Organizations can create and foster productive ways to learn through these methods:

- *Culture:* The culture of an organization includes its shared values, beliefs, assumptions, customs, and practices. Successful organizations realize that learning is an essential ingredient in success. They make learning a habit and integrate it into all organizational functions.

- *Vision:* Organizations must develop a broad, clear vision of where they want to go. A desire for a future in which employees are encouraged to learn about and experiment with ways to deliver better products and services needs to be part of that vision.

- *Strategy:* The tactics, methods, and action plans an organization uses to achieve its vision should include strategies for the collection, transferal, and use of knowledge in every area of the organization.

- *Structure:* Organizations should be streamlined so that employees are not limited by artificial boundaries. The organization should encourage contact, information flow, local responsibility, and especially collaboration among all employees.

Systems Thinking

Systems thinking encourages a holistic view—where specific situations are considered in the context of the larger whole. It looks below events to the patterns and structures that created them—just like the chaos and complexity theory. The model for systems thinking promoted by Peter Senge (Titcomb 1998), founding chairperson of the Society for Organizational Learning and a senior lecturer at the Massachusetts Institute of Technology, and others usually involves developing graphs of what happens in an organization. This model characterizes recurring feedback loops as system archetypes, which are generic configurations that fit many situations.

Including perspectives of the chaos and complexity theory in systems thinking reveals the limitations of models. Many graphical representations of systems make them seem simple, linear, and predictable. Yet human systems are relentlessly nonlinear. The challenge is finding their connections, patterns, and underlying order.

Pros and Cons

Using the chaos and complexity theory to understand an organization has advantages despite its similarity to the management practices of learning organizations and systems thinking and its relative newness in OD. And, as with any new organizational theory, chaos and complexity theory has attracted its share of criticism.

Pros

These are some of the pros of using the chaos and complexity theory:

- *Flexibility:* By defining, in broad terms, the direction an organization should take or what it should accomplish and then allowing employees to discover the best ways to get there creates a culture that allows an organization to adapt quickly to change. Rather than imposing a process from above that is difficult to change, employees can continue working toward the overall goal with a minimum of disruption.

- *Creativity:* Although managers may have more experience in their particular business than the employees, people are naturally creative. Surprising ideas can come from anyone. When managers allow employees to design their own course of action, each person's unique life experiences can shape and improve a process in ways that management could never conceive. In addition, employees who shape their own processes are more motivated because their involvement fosters a sense of ownership in the organization's mission.

- *Stability:* Although it may seem odd to list stability as a quality of complex systems, they are actually quite stable due to the interconnectedness of their parts. A large system made up of smaller parts is more stable than a single, large system because of the many checks and balances that exist among the various parts.

- *Leverage:* Systems thinking shows that change can be surprisingly easy if one identifies the right connections. Leveraging a small effort can cause enormous results that would make no sense if one looked only at the results in terms of cause and effect. The key is to find connections between the parts that should change and alter them in ways that will bring them in line with established objectives.

Cons

These are some of the cons of using the chaos and complexity theory:

- *It's too new:* Some people worry that chaos and complexity is just another entry in a long line of management fads that have entered and stirred up the workplace—often with little or no improvement to show for the efforts of employees and managers. Others see it as nothing more than a new take on systems thinking. Naturally, these battle-scarred veterans of previous management theories will be wary of chaos and complexity until it has proven itself with well-known and respected organizations.

- *It's too soon:* Many theorists and academics question whether the chaos and complexity theory is ready to be applied to social systems, such as work organizations. They call, not surprisingly, for more study and scholarly discussion before subjecting organizations to the rigors of another management theory. The divergent view is that the only way to further develop and prove that the chaos and complexity theory is valid and beneficial is to apply it to actual organizations.

- *It's too simple:* Although many scientists and mathematicians feel that chaos and complexity cannot be explained accurately in simple, nontechnical terms, people with limited exposure to these disciplines can grasp the fundamentals as they relate to organizations. Although there can be a danger to oversimplifying the concepts (which take time, effort, and a solid background in math and physics to understand completely), a simplified version allows individuals to determine if the chaos and complexity theory would benefit their organization. They can then make an informed decision as to whether to delve into it fully.

- *It's too complex:* The study of complex systems has evolved from a number of disciplines (for example, physics, math, biology, and computer science), and there is no single comprehensive theory that covers all of its principles. In addition, much of what had been written is highly technical and inaccessible to those without a solid background in the sciences, including most people with an interest in applying it to organizations. Confusion is bound to result when a theory about understanding and creating order and simplified structures is called *chaos and complexity*.

Many, most notably Margaret Wheatley, management consultant and author of *Leadership and the New Science* (1994) and *A Simpler Way* (Wheatley and Kellner-Rogers 1996), suggest that members of organizations should be allowed to form their own self-directed systems with only a few guidelines or rules imposed by management as part of a broad vision of where the organization is headed.

One roadblock to implementing programs such as these, however, has been the highly technical nature of most of the material published on chaos and complexity. Also, managers and employees alike are weary after years of trying to understand the latest buzzwords and adapt to the latest management fads. Although these concerns are certainly valid—who has the time or energy for *another* management system, and a confusing one at that—chaos and complexity theory is so different from previous models that it is worth considering.

Although it is always risky to see any new management theory as the answer, the chaos and complexity theory can give managers a better sense of how organizations work as a whole. This increased understanding could help them become more effective leaders of change.

Similarities and Differences Between Chaos and Complexity

To apply the chaos and complexity theory to organizational management, learning organization expert Mike McMasters (Titcomb 1998) has developed applicable definitions.

Chaos is a state where patterns cannot be made nor details understood. Chaos is the result of an organization resisting change and then reaching a point where change is unavoidable. At this point, change occurs rapidly and can take a system in unexpected directions. Eventually, the system either reorganizes itself in a viable state or disintegrates.

Complex systems have details, whose role in the larger system cannot be understood fully by examining them apart from the system. By carefully studying the whole system, patterns can be identified.

OD Intervention

The chaos and complexity theory emerged from scientific discoveries that the universe and natural phenomena are composed of chaotic, dynamic, complex systems rather than predictable, law-abiding structures. Experts have applied these theories to organizations as a new way to understand the complex, dynamic, nonlinear systems that are today's organizations (Wheatley 1994). Although many employees continue to work in the Newtonian, hierarchical structure, they feel the chaotic complexity of change swirling about them. Chaos—"a state where patterns cannot be made nor details understood"—is a familiar experience for many employees working in settings where change is resisted until it becomes unavoidable, and then it occurs at a rapid, disorienting pace (Titcomb 1998). The paradox is, however, that from within chaos emerges order—repeated patterns that have coherence and can be recognized.

Organization and management practitioners and visionaries, such as Dee Hock (Durrance 1997) and Margaret Wheatley (1994), suggest this new scientific theory of the universe offers insight for the leadership and organization of work. Internal consultants at the front line of chaotic change in organizations have opportunities to apply these concepts in their organizations. Some initial steps might be to

- encourage managers to loosen control and allow teams to self-organize

- promote a search for alternative or innovative solutions rather than clinging to past practices

- engage the whole system to participate in planning, problem solving, and creating the future

- help develop and communicate shared values and purpose throughout the organization.

People often note that in today's business environment, nothing is as certain as change. Unfortunately, people usually do not like change. But with technology driving organizations at a frenetic pace, leaders must be more skillful than ever in the art of change management. Although much has been written regarding this topic, it can be boiled down to its basic elements—the four Cs of change: create, communicate, connect, and congratulate.

Create

As with any initiative, the first step involves creating a vision. Leaders must identify the major pitfalls and benefits of the journey and then enlist senior management to join in. It's essential that they buy in to the need for change, understand what the change is, and be willing to do what it takes to achieve success.

Communicate

After the core team has been formed and everyone is on board, it is time to communicate to the larger population. This will take careful planning. A cross-functional team should be created to draw up the communication plan; a strategy mapped out that ensures no group is left out; and the most effective media, messages, and messenger identified for each stage. Communication should be frequent and come in various packages, including email, video, print, meetings, contests, meals, and voicemail. Constant reminders are helpful so that the group never loses sight of where the organization is going and the benefits waiting for them.

Connect

There are many things WLP professionals can do to connect with the organization's population. They can make it personal, get up from the desk and out of the office, and go out and talk to people and find out what's on their minds. Where are things going well, and where do they need some help? What would they do differently? What obstacles can be removed? What resources can be provided? The road to change shouldn't be a lockstep march. Rather it will be full of twists and turns. WLP professionals should not wait to find out from senior managers when these things need attention, because it will be too late. Thus WLP professionals need to go out and have informal chats or invite a few folks to lunch or coffee. The information received will more than compensate for the meal and time, and it will make the final implementation richer.

Congratulate

Change is not always easy nor is it neat and clean. Morale is key to the life of the initiative, so WLP professionals need to pay attention to what people are doing, set them up to have small successes early on and reward them publicly, and make sure to celebrate all of the milestones along the way.

Creating the right environment for change takes work, careful planning, and a bit of luck. However, if done well, the rewards for the organization and its employees can be immeasurable.

✓ Chapter 2 Knowledge Check

1. **Which of the following terms is most appropriately defined as the study of how simple systems can generate complicated behavior and is a state where patterns cannot be made nor details understood?**

    __ **A.** Complexity

    __ **B.** Chaos

    __ **C.** The butterfly effect

    __ **D.** The whole is more than the parts

2. **Which of the following states that the central premise as it relates to organizations is that order can emerge out of chaos?**

    __ **A.** Complexity

    __ **B.** Chaos

    __ **C.** The butterfly effect

    __ **D.** The whole is more than the parts

3. **Which of the following is *not* an example of the pros of using the chaos and complexity theory?**

    __ **A.** Leverage

    __ **B.** Rigidity

    __ **C.** Creativity

    __ **D.** Stability

4. **Which of the following encourages a holistic approach so that changes or initiatives in one component of an organization do not negatively affect another part of the organization?**

    __ **A.** System archetypes

    __ **B.** Stability

    __ **C.** Recurring feedback loops

    __ **D.** Systems thinking

5. **Which of the following best describes how the chaos theory relates to organizational change?**

    ___ **A.** The best way to understand a system and chaos is to break it down into smaller, more manageable chunks and examine one component at a time.

    ___ **B.** Chaos is the result of many details in a larger system that cannot be fully understood by examining them apart from the system.

    ___ **C.** Chaos is the result of an organizational system resisting change and then reaching a point where change is unavoidable. At this point, change occurs rapidly and can take the system into unexpected directions.

    ___ **D.** Chaos is the result of an organizational system that is made up of a limited number of repeated patterns that can be examined to see certain behaviors and qualities begin and appear again and again.

6. **Although theorists do not agree on which characteristics are most important with regard to chaotic and complex systems, most accept several characteristics as the central part of the chaos and complexity theory. These characteristics include all *but which* of the following?**

    ___ **A.** Problem events within a system are usually microcosms of the chaos within it, and dissecting an individual event reveals the key issue of the organization.

    ___ **B.** Complex systems have multiple causes and effects that are not linked in time and space, so isolating and examining one action may provide an inaccurate perception.

    ___ **C.** All complex systems are made up of a limited number of repeating patterns, and, that although they may appear to occur randomly, a closer look reveals that these patterns do repeat again and again.

    ___ **D.** The whole is more than the parts, meaning that the best way to understand a complex system is to break it down into smaller, more manageable parts and see how each component interacts with other components.

7. **Learning organizations accept the fact that nothing is always stable and that they must be prepared to quickly change their strategies to adapt.**

    ___ **A.** True

    ___ **B.** False

8. **Organizations creating a successful environment for change should focus on creating a vision, communicating the plan, connecting with people, and congratulating on successes.**

    ___ **A.** True

    ___ **B.** False

9. **An internal change consultant is working with the managers to agree to loosen their control and allow teams to self-organize. Which theory is the consultant using to help facilitate change in this organization?**

___ **A.** Equity theory

___ **B.** Goal setting theory

___ **C.** Motivation theory

___ **D.** Chaos and complexity theory

10. **What is the order for the four Cs of change?**

___ **A.** Communicate, Create, Connect, Congratulate

___ **B.** Congratulate, Connect, Communicate, Create

___ **C.** Create, Communicate, Connect, Congratulate

___ **D.** Connect, Create, Congratulate, Communicate

References

Durrance, B. (April 1997). "The Evolutionary Vision of Dee Hock." *T&D*, pp. 24–31.

Roos, J. (February 1997). "The Poised Organization: Navigating Effectively on Knowledge Landscapes." *The Strategy & Complexity Seminal.* London: London School of Economics.

Scott, B. (2000). *Consulting on the Inside.* Alexandria, VA: ASTD.

Titcomb, T.J. (1998). "Chaos and Complexity Theory." *Infoline* No. 259807.

Wheatley, M. (1994). *Leadership and the New Science.* San Francisco: Berrett-Koehler.

Wheatley, M., and M. Kellner-Rogers. (1996). *A Simpler Way.* San Francisco: Berrett-Koehler.

3
Appreciative Inquiry Theory

Appreciative inquiry theory is an approach to large-scale organizational change that involves the analysis of positive and successful (rather than negative or failing) operations. The appreciative inquiry *4-D cycle* (discovery, dream, design, destiny) includes identifying problems, analyzing causes, searching for solutions, and developing an action plan. The organization development (OD) professional can make use of the description of best practices as a way to initiate organizational change. How these stories are collected and interpreted is central to the appropriate use of this theory.

Learning Objectives:

- ☑ Explain how appreciative inquiry applies to leading groups or teams.
- ☑ List and describe effective questioning techniques.
- ☑ Describe the effect of a multidisciplinary situation on the change initiative's success.
- ☑ Define experiential activities and how they expand learning.
- ☑ Explain how using appreciative inquiry affects organizational realignment.

Background

Appreciative inquiry theory is an affirmative approach to personal and organization transformation. The appreciative inquiry approach is based on the assumption that positive questions and conversations about visions, values, successes, and strengths have the power to enliven possibilities and engage people in creating exciting new realities.

David Cooperrider, Suresh Srivastva, and their colleagues at Case Western Reserve University developed appreciative inquiry in the 1980s. According to Cooperrider, Whitney, and Stavros (2003), the aim of appreciative inquiry is to help the organization in

- envisioning a collectively desired future

- carrying forth that vision in ways that successfully translate intention into reality and beliefs into practices.

At the core of appreciative inquiry is a belief that reality is socially constructed—that the world is created in conversation. When conversations focus on strengths, possibilities, and vision, the reality is more likely positive and inspirational. When conversations focus on problems, complaints, and weaknesses, those things become more prominent and real. According to the appreciative inquiry approach, if the OD practitioner and the client take a problem-solving approach to change, this limits their ability to create a new and exciting future. The appreciative inquiry approach focuses on opportunities and possibilities, not problems. By having open and positive conversations about success and what is possible, solutions can produce more desirable results.

For the OD practitioner, appreciative inquiry is an approach that can be used in a variety of consulting and coaching situations, including change solutions and general facilitation. Appreciative inquiry creates a context for inclusion and participation and can transform traditional hierarchical organizations into workplaces characterized by collaboration, engagement, and partnership. Appreciative inquiry can help managers transition from an authoritarian to a more empowering style because it is participative and inclusive. It is also useful for helping to renew and reengage professionals who have been stuck in a routine.

Appreciative inquiry is an approach that shifts the focus of analysis and dialog from problems and concerns to opportunities and visions. Appreciative inquiry uses research, feedback, action planning, and action to implement robust change solutions. The difference is what's being looked at and talked about. Problems still exist and are acknowledged when using an appreciative inquiry approach, but they are framed to focus on what's possible in the future. For example, a problem of high turnover would become an inquiry into what being an employer of choice might look like. A problem of long product-development cycles would become an inquiry that explores product-development strengths and the creation of a vision for world-class product development. These may seem like subtle changes, but they are not. Shifting the focus and conversation to the affirmative opens up participation and creativity. Appreciative inquiry unleashes employees' passion and power.

So, is appreciative inquiry a touchy-feely approach? Not at all. It is a powerful tool that can improve business productivity and results. In fact, OD practitioners who use appreciative inquiry find that the approach can yield effective results, sometimes even more quickly than other problem-solving approaches. Appreciative inquiry engages participants and produces more and better ideas and cuts down on resistance to change. The appreciative inquiry approach honors current strengths and builds upon them to help participants build a vision and plan for the future.

Leading Groups or Teams

An affirmative approach to change, like that of appreciative inquiry, generates more ideas about what's possible and reduces resistance to change. Appreciative inquiry is an approach that requires inclusion. Appreciative inquiry solutions will be more successful if all employees (and maybe even vendors or customers) participate in the process. In general, more and broader perspectives are better. Because the appreciative inquiry process is inclusive, it reduces resistance to changes that might occur later.

Using Appreciative Inquiry

OD practitioners unfamiliar with appreciative inquiry should not attempt a large-scale appreciative inquiry solution. Appreciative inquiry can be used in a variety of situations such as

- coaching one-on-one
- planning strategically
- planning meetings
- strengthening relationships
- reframing problem-solving efforts
- enhancing decisions
- generating new ideas
- training classes
- benchmarking organizations
- engaging vendors or customers
- increasing employee satisfaction
- launching new project teams.

OD practitioners can begin using the appreciative inquiry approach by adding affirmative questions to their coaching, consulting, and facilitating and getting people talking about what interests them the most—their ideas, hopes, and proudest moments. The workplace learning and performance (WLP) professional will want to practice reframing problem statements and helping people articulate their vision. Here are several sample questions:

Coaching

- When have you been most interested and engaged in your work?
- What do you value most about yourself and your work?

Consulting

- What is special about this organization?
- In what ways is the company best in its class?
- What do you hope will have taken place in five years?

Facilitating

- If there were no constraints in people, time, or money, what approach would you take?
- What does a home run in performance look like?
- What special talents does the team have that will help the company meet its goals in the future?

Appreciative inquiry is a powerful approach to change and OD. It creates an environment that engages and excites people, but it is also very pragmatic and business oriented. By shifting conversations to the affirmative, appreciative inquiry can help businesses grow and improve in ways that inspire those involved. OD practitioners should continuously build their knowledge of appreciative inquiry and its wide-ranging applications.

Effective Questioning Techniques

A common way to begin a change process is to look at what is not working and start solving the problem. This process can become negative and limit options. Appreciative inquiry questions are positive, hopeful, and focused on successes and what is possible. Appreciative inquiry questions leave people feeling confident, excited, and creative.

The 4-D Cycle

David Cooperrider and Suresh Srivastva developed the 4-D cycle to guide OD practitioners and clients through the appreciative inquiry approach. The 4-D cycle can be used for large or small solutions. OD practitioners can even use the 4-D cycle when coaching individuals and teams. The elements of the 4-D cycle are shown in figure 3-1.

Topic

The appreciative inquiry approach starts with identifying the topic that the team will discuss and reinvent. The OD practitioner and the client should carefully select the topic, because this sets the tone for the inquiry. The topic should be something important to the company and an area that, if improved, would make a big difference. To select the topic, the following question should be answered: *What do we want to do more of?* Some sample topics are

- making the company the employer of choice
- speeding up the product-development process
- delighting customers
- streaming new revenue
- envisioning ideas for growth
- producing quality products
- innovating service.

Good topics focus the conversation in a positive and powerful way and communicate what's important. Topics should be desirable, stimulating, and related to the organization's future. Table 3-1 shows several examples of how to reframe problems into excellent appreciative inquiry topics.

Figure 3-1. The 4-D Cycle

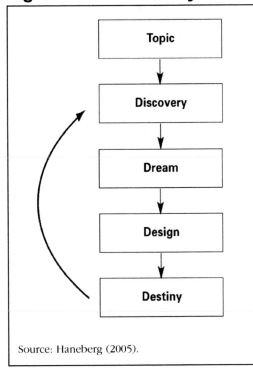

Source: Haneberg (2005).

Discovery

The OD practitioner conducts appreciative interviews that uncover current best practices, strengths, and strategic capabilities. The appreciative interview—an important part of the appreciative approach—asks participants to recall successes, high points, and times of full engagement related to the topic. The interviewer (often the OD practitioner) will also ask about learning experiences and visions, and how an optimal future would look.

To plan for the interviews, the OD practitioner will need to prepare an introduction of the topic and construct the interview questions. Creating great questions is important, so the OD practitioner should research appreciative inquiry questions and review sample interviews. Depending on the size of the appreciative inquiry solution, the OD practitioner may need to train additional interviewers.

Appreciative interviews may be done one-on-one or in group meetings. The discovery phase of appreciative inquiry kick-starts positive conversations about the topic and generates constructive stories about the organization's strengths and successes. It prepares the organization for the rest of the appreciative inquiry process. Here are some example appreciative inquiry interview questions:

Table 3-1. Defining Problems as Opportunities

Problem Statement	Opportunity
Turnover is too high.	How can we create a work environment that attracts and retains the best talent?
Projects are not getting done on time.	How can we master project success, implementation, execution, and results?
Our customer base is not growing fast enough to support new product introductions.	Who are our customers of today and tomorrow, and how can we find and build a relationship with them?
Our costs are out of line with revenues and need to be cut.	What is the model of optimal efficiency and alignment for our organization?
Our employees do not have the needed skills and are not performing up to expectations.	How can we create a learning organization where employees grow and help the organization respond to change needs?

- Tell me about how you came to work for this company. What attracted you to the position, and what were your hopes for what you would achieve?

- We all have special talents and contribute to the company's success. What are your special skills and talents?

- Describe an experience that you enjoyed and would consider one of the high points since working for this company.

- What two or three changes would make this company the best it can be in terms of results and being a great place to work?

- Every company has special strengths and capabilities. What's special about this company?

Dream

The dream phase of appreciative inquiry is a participative discovery of what's possible. Participants explore and discuss their visions, hopes, ideas, and dreams for the future. The OD practitioner, or other facilitator, will lead large-group discussions that help participants explore hopes and dreams for work, relationships, and organizational goals. Together, they think big and beyond where they have in the past. Boundaries are broken, and anything is possible.

The goal of the dream phase is to create a powerful and amazing vision for the future related to the topic. For example, the vision might be the best way to create and execute projects or to create a partnership with customers in new product development. The vision could also relate to the internal workings of the organization, like how to build cross-functional relationships and creative communities. To enable the best outcome, the OD practitioner or facilitator will want to employ methods that enliven creativity and participation. Table 3-2 lists example questions to address during the dream phase.

Design

The work done thus far is synthesized into a picture or model of what should change. Depending on the topic, this might mean creating a new organization plan, a set of operating practices, or a process map. Participants consider the organization's strengths and vision statement and determine how this should affect the structure, roles, processes, development, and practices. The design phase is a time to remain creative and optimistic while considering how to realign various parts of the organization to the new vision for the future.

The output of the design phase is a view of the desired state expressed in powerful statements called ***provocative proposition***s. Here is how Cooperrider, Whitney, and Stavros (2003) describe them:

> A provocative proposition is a statement that bridges the best of "what is" with your own speculation or intuition of "what might be." It is provocative to the extent to which it stretches the realm of the status quo, challenges common assumptions or routines, and helps suggest real possibilities that represent desired possibilities for the organization and its people.

Destiny

This phase correlates with both the action planning and the action phases of action research (action research is discussed in the following chapter). Participants celebrate what they have created and set actions and projects in motion to make the vision a reality. Project teams may be assigned to make specific changes or to investigate options and approaches. Additional appreciative inquiry projects may also be spawned.

The destiny phase continues the positive momentum and allows highly motivated people to create the future they envisioned. The OD practitioner and the client must be mind-

Table 3-2. Dream Phase Questions

Example Appreciative Inquiry Dream Phase Questions
Project your thinking out five years (adjust number of years to fit the topic). This company has been extremely successful in exceeding its vision and goals, what does this future look like?
How is the company viewed in the marketplace?
What will it be like to work here in the future?
How is the organization structured? How is work done?
Describe the organization culture that is in place.

ful of the support structure that will be needed to ensure the work remains at the front of peoples' minds and lists of priorities. Another goal of the destiny phase is to expand the use of the appreciative inquiry approach throughout the organization. There is a self-reinforcing nature of using positive and affirmative inquiry to improve the business.

The 4-D cycle starts with dreams and ends with substantive changes in the organization's practices, processes, systems, and structures. Like action research, appreciative inquiry is an approach that is self-correcting and iterative. OD practitioners who try appreciative inquiry must be ready to see the process and outcomes take on lives of their own. The outcome cannot be determined up front. This is the case any time inclusion, participation, and creativity are maximized. That the outcome cannot be predicted should not dissuade a person from trying appreciative inquiry; the results are generally better and more interesting than can be imagined.

Open- and Closed-Ended Questions

Using questioning techniques often stimulates discussion and helps to check for understanding. These are several types of questioning techniques:

- ***Open-ended:*** These types of questions stimulate discussion. Open questions have no one specific correct answer and encourage individuals to draw on their own experiences and apply them to the current situation or discussion. These questions require more than one-word answers, enabling individuals to express their thoughts, feelings, ideas, and opinions. Some examples include "What experiences can you share about . . . " or "How would you . . . " or "How might you use this information?" The primary function of this type of question is to *explore*.

- ***Closed-ended:*** Also known as direct questions, these questions help to check for understanding or to test for consensus. These are sometimes preferable to open-ended questions to limit information. They are excellent for getting at specific facts or information and directing the individual's mind to a specific, verifiable bit of knowledge or experience. "What is your name?" is an example of a closed-ended question or any questions where individuals would answer with a yes or no. The primary focus of this type of question is to *focus*.

The act of asking questions of an organization or group influences the group in some way. According to Cooperrider, "change starts with the first question," and not at some distant point in the future when implementation occurs. Therefore, considering the questions to ask is important.

In *Appreciative Inquiry: Change at the Speed of Imagination,* Jane Magruder Watkins and Bernard J. Mohr (2001) give an example of framing language. If an organization chooses to focus on "increasing customer satisfaction," practitioners have a choice between asking traditional questions or asking positively framed questions. These are some examples:

Traditional

- "What are we doing to cause customer dissatisfaction?"
- "What do we need to do to decrease customer dissatisfaction?"

Positive

- "When have our customers been really happy and satisfied with the company? What were we doing then that we can build on?"
- "How can we create an exceptional customer service experience?"

Multidisciplinary Learning Topics

Now that the path has been broadly defined to the ideal state, the next step is to determine the details of how to get there. In the solution selection, design, and development stage, the initiatives will evolve to create the future state.

Solution selection, design, and development require teams to co-create the future. This is a continuation of the whole system change process and is critical for ensuring that the solution meets the needs of those most affected by it. Solutions include

- training
- knowledge capture and management
- job aids
- electronic performance support systems
- job analysis
- work design solutions
- mentoring and coaching
- feedback
- compensation plans
- health and wellness initiatives
- performance appraisals
- *leadership development*.

Note that paths to the ideal future state may require a combination of many solutions. Teams may also need to work with subject matter experts (SMEs) to get to the future state. The following section focuses specifically on experiential activities to achieve the ideal future state.

Experiential Activities to Expand Learning

Humans learn best by doing. Implementing a change initiative is no different—participants must be involved in the process to truly implement a change initiative. Many trainers believe that the only way someone is going to learn a skill is by doing it in a real or a simulated environment. In addition, plenty of structured and easily available learning resources are integral to this approach, without the benefit of a trainer standing over the learner's shoulder.

Pedagogists have been using this process for years and have termed it ***discovery learning***. The indicator of learning in this method is the learners' ability to do something after the training that they could not do before. This change in ability is often more intellectual than physical and, therefore, harder to measure. For example, people might build skills as presenters through discovery by learning how to think on their feet during arguments. The skill change is in the facilitation ability, but it is a mental change occurring internally that has caused it.

Experiential learning occurs when a learner participates in an activity, reviews the activity, identifies useful knowledge or skills that were gained, and transfers the result to the workplace. An American baseball player, Vernon Sanders Law, stated that "Experience is a hard teacher because she gives the test first, the lesson after." This is the learning process in day-to-day life—life experience.

Experiential learning activities (ELAs) attempt to duplicate life experience. Participants experience what they are to learn before they discuss it.

ELAs are based on several characteristics:

- They are directed toward a specific learning goal.
- They are structured; that is, they have specific steps and a process that must be followed to ensure results.
- There is a high degree of participant involvement.
- They generate data and information for participant analysis.
- They require processing or debriefing for maximum learning.

The steps in Pfeiffer and Jones' experiential learning cycle explain what must occur during an activity to ensure maximum learning occurs (1975). The five steps are experiencing, publishing, processing, generalizing, and applying.

Step 1. Experiencing: Do Something

This is the step that is associated with the game or fun of the experience. Participants are involved in completing a defined task. If the process ends here, all learning is left to chance, and the trainer has not completed the task.

Step 2. Publishing: Share Observations

The second step of the cycle gives the learners a chance to share what they saw, how they felt, and what they experienced. The trainer can facilitate this in several ways: record data in the large group, have participants share or interview in subgroups, or lead a variation of a round-robin. These are questions the facilitator may ask:

- What happened? What did you observe?

- What occurred during the activity?

- How did you feel about this?

The facilitator typically begins with a broad question and then focuses on more specific questions. The facilitator may probe for turning points or decisions that affected the outcome. This stage is important because it allows the participants to vent or express strong emotions, and it allows the facilitator to gather data.

Step 3. Processing: Interpret Dynamics or Concepts

This step gives the participants a chance to discuss the patterns and dynamics they observed during the activity. Observers may be used to discussing this step. These are questions the facilitator may ask:

- Why do you think that may have occurred?

- What did you learn about yourself?

- What did you learn?

- What theories or principles may be true based on your experience?

The facilitator will again begin with broad questions and then focus on more specific questions. This stage allows participants to test hypotheses, preparing them to apply what they learned. This stage allows the facilitator a way to observe how much participants learned from the experience.

Step 4. Generalizing: Connect to Real Life

The key question in this step is "So what?" Participants are led to focus their awareness on situations that are similar to what they have experienced. This step makes the activity practical. Facilitators may ask these questions:

- How does this relate to . . . ?

- What did you learn about yourself?

- What does this suggest to you about . . . ?

- How does this experience help you understand . . . ?

- What if . . . ?

This stage ensures that the participants grasp the learning that was intended. The "what if" question becomes a bridge to the last step, which is application.

Step 5. Applying: Plan Effective Change

The last step presents the reason the activity was conducted: "Now what?" The facilitator helps participants apply generalizations to actual situations in which they are involved. The group may establish goals, contract for change, make promises, identify potential workplace changes, or initiate any other actions that result from the experience. These are the questions that are asked:

- What will you do differently as a result of this experience?
- How will you transfer this learning to the workplace?
- How and when will you apply your learning?
- How may this help you in the future?
- What's next?

Participants frequently follow this step with an action plan or at least spend some time noting their thoughts about how life may be different as a result of the ELA.

The ELA is a powerful tool available to facilitators. It is time-consuming and, therefore, used sparingly. There shouldn't be any shortcuts taken when facilitating an ELA. The value is truly in the process.

Tips for Facilitating Activities

Activities are potent learning tools for participants as long as the facilitator is prepared and follows a few suggestions for conducting them. These tips for introducing, supporting, and processing activities will help the facilitator think through all of the nuances of facilitating activities.

Introducing Activities

Ensuring that each activity gets started efficiently is critical. A facilitator can use these steps to ensure that happens prior to the group's starting an activity or an ELA:

- Provide brief, general instructions, including whether they will need materials, pens, and so on.
- Establish a clear objective that positions the activity within the context of the training module or session.
- Do not provide too much information if the intent is for the participants to discover an "aha!"
- Use a process to help participants form small groups before providing more specific instructions so that participants do not forget what they heard in the first place.

- After participants are settled in to their working groups, ascertain that everyone is focused and attentive. Then provide more specific direction.

- Tell participants how much involvement is expected of them. Depending on the activity, consider telling them what will happen after. Will they be expected to share scores with the larger group? Will they be working in the same group? Will there be a large-group discussion?

- Distribute additional materials that may be required and demonstrate any processes that are necessary.

- Announce the amount of time the activity will require. It is a good idea to post the time on a flipchart so it is visible to all. If the activity has steps within the process, post a schedule of how much time should be spent on each step. Suggest any roles that may make the activity move smoothly: timekeeper, recorder, or spokesperson.

- Ensure that everyone knows what to do; ask if anyone has any questions.

- Circulate among the groups to ensure that everyone understands the activity.

Supporting Activities

Facilitators can be quiet guides to ensure that participants are successful with their activities. Facilitators will walk among the groups to ensure that everyone understands the task, stays on track, and reaches the end. Note that this would actually occur during the activity or step 1 of an ELA.

- During the activity, remind participants of the rules, if necessary.

- Give a "time is half up" signal and a "five minutes left" or a "one minute left" signal. Abrupt commands of "stop" or "time is up" may prevent participants from achieving the goal.

- Make suggestions about the process. Take care, however, not to give away the answer. Suggesting, rather than commanding, allows participants to maintain control of the situation.

- Walk among participants to identify confusion, problems, questions, and time needed to complete the task.

- Adjust time, if necessary, and announce to the group but only if all the groups need more or less time. Allowing some groups to have more time when others finished within the time limit will be perceived as unfair.

- Be sure to debrief the activity at its conclusion.

Processing Activities

This is probably the most important part of the activity. When conducting an ELA, the facilitator should be addressing the questions and working through the process included in steps 2, 3, 4, and 5. Otherwise, the facilitator should assist the learners to understand the implications of what they just experienced or completed and help them address the importance and the relevance of the activity to themselves personally. The facilitator can use these suggestions:

- Relate the activity to previous as well as future training modules.

- Maintain a facilitative role without one-upping participants' experiences. Add information if it is a tip or technique that will be useful for participants to understand the content or to improve a skill. However, if the facilitator can add that information at another time, save it until then.

- Share pertinent observations made during the exercise.

- Avoid teaching, preaching, or lecturing.

- Stress practical application.

- Correct only when participants have obviously come to incorrect solutions, and then use either a questioning technique or participation from other groups to make the correction.

- Debriefing is required so that learning outcomes can be discussed. Record comments on a flipchart.

- Use representatives from each group to conduct the debriefing.

- Even if participants disagree on the outcome, ensure a common understanding among the group of what occurred before moving on.

Organizational Realignment

In terms of appreciative inquiry, when organizational issues must be addressed, alignment regarding goals and outcomes sought, and the measures of success determined, an OD practitioner may want to create a provocative proposition. This approach describes and captures the energy of the organization and offers an exciting possibility for members to create. Examples of this approach include organizational creeds, such as, "Our customers have a pleasant experience when they talk to us" or "The information we need to answer their questions is available to us at the touch of a finger." It is also important to continue to reinforce the client's personal learning and increasing self-knowledge and to emphasize the value of processes or structures to build organizational learning. It is important to clarify expectations and needs before finalizing plans and agendas.

The implementation of new structures and processes is critical to the success of the realignment. To ensure that team members and peers support the new way of doing the work, an OD practitioner should do the following:

- Work with management and the human resources function on the timing of the plan's implementation, especially if any individual jobs or positions are affected.

- Coach the client, the managers, and the team members on ways to communicate the vision, realignment plan, transition plan, and role of each team member. They also need to share the plan with peers and gain their support. Timing of communications is critical. If an individual's job is changing significantly, the managers should talk to that person one-on-one before any team announcements occur.

The communication plan should include

- a rollout or general announcement

- a clear plan for the transition of roles and processes

- daily or weekly progress chats as needed.

The client, managers, team members, and OD practitioner should be available and ready to listen to any concerns, suggestions, or questions.

WLP professionals need to be flexible enough to accept that the plan may need to be altered; take time every day to check in with the client and the design team; and avoid micromanaging the process, but show support and invite feedback.

As the realignment rolls out and takes hold, it is important to monitor and measure performance and productivity. After all, that is why changes were made in the first place. Measures should be communicated clearly and discussed often. Key measures and milestones should be posted in a visible place in the department.

In an aligned organization, disorder is reduced and the work environment is more intrinsically motivating. It runs like a well-oiled machine. To ensure the organization stays aligned, it needs to be evaluated regularly and as changes occur. Although some elements of the system always need realignment, it is a good idea to evaluate the overall alignment of departments every two years, and then follow up with smaller redesign efforts as needed. For example, if a company launches a new product line, a portion of the department's work, processes, and roles may need realignment.

How to Build Courses

Once the path to the ideal state has been defined broadly, the next step is to determine the details of how to get to this future state. In other words, solution selection, design, and development describe the initiatives that will evolve to optimize the future state. There is no prescribed methodology and plenty of choices.

Solution selection, design, and development involve teams to determine the best route. It's important to note that the WLP practitioner does not prescribe the solution. Instead, he or she works with the organizational team to co-create the future they jointly imagine. This is a continuation of the whole system change process and is critical to ensuring that the solution meets the needs of those most affected by it.

Most descriptions of the future state require several solutions from various categories. For example, an organization may decide to implement a new software system to enhance its distribution of products to the customer. Although orders are already received within five days, customers often need the product much sooner than five days. New distribution software could get products to the customer within one business day, if needed. New distribution software is a complex project, and many solutions are essential. To accomplish this future state, the organization would probably require

- collaboration
- financial forecasting
- capital investment and spending
- information systems
- reengineering
- value engineering
- interface design
- job redesign
- work methods
- quality control, management, and assurance
- documentation and standards
- on-the-job training
- job aids
- incentives and rewards
- communication—newsletters, announcements, and so on.

Solution selection, design, and development use a three-step process. First, the future state team, including SMEs and the WLP professional, determine what solutions are essential for success. Then, the future state team and SMEs design each initiative and the project management plan to accomplish the solution, while interfacing with the other solutions. Then, each initiative needs to be developed in detail. It is easy to see that the actual distribution software development is only one of many aspects of this future state project.

Once the future state is designed, the stage is set for implementation. This is not a lock-step situation. For instance, communication will begin prior to distribution software completion. In fact, financial analysis and forecasting will probably be the first step. Interface design and value engineering will be early initiatives to determine if the future state will provide the expected value to the organization. In most cases, destiny or solution implementation occurs gradually as each initiative takes shape.

Initiatives need to be coordinated so that there is sufficient interface and collaboration. The future state team needs to ensure that there is sufficient process consulting with the related departments so that the future state will fit in well with production, purchasing, sales, marketing, and so on. Employees throughout the organization will need to be informed and many prepared through communication, formal training, or on-the-job training. The future state team will need to communicate progress, network with all of the affected departments, and form alliances, such as between production and sales so that sales representatives can inform customers of the new distribution timeframe. There will also need to be trial runs to remove any problems prior to the final start date. Because future state projects are often expensive and essential to the organization's long-term viability, it is important to evaluate them to demonstrate results and value-added. Three types of evaluation are important for an appreciative inquiry effort:

1. ***Formative evaluation*** begins with performance analysis—questioning whether the methods used are best for this effort, the right people are involved, the right data analysis tools are used, and so on. This questioning continues throughout the entire appreciative inquiry effort.

2. ***Summative evaluation*** begins to summarize results based on immediate reaction of initiative implementation. Do those involved believe that things are going well? Does the initiative seem right? Is any correction necessary at this point? Do the first results match the expected future state?

3. ***Confirmative evaluation*** provides the intermediate and long-term information to demonstrate that the desired future state is occurring. Continuing results are measured against expected results. Continuing effectiveness is measured to determine if the results are making a positive contribution to the organization. Finally, return-on-investment is monitored to be certain that the expenditures and efforts justify the cost in human, financial, and capital resources.

✓ Chapter 3 Knowledge Check

1. Which of the following uses data collection in the form of collecting people's stories of something at its best by structuring questions and information to focus on the positive to initiate organizational change?

   __ **A.** Action research

   __ **B.** Neurolinguistic programming

   __ **C.** Chaos and complexity theory

   __ **D.** Appreciative inquiry theory

2. Cooperrider and Srivastva developed the 4-D cycle, which includes discovery, dream, design, and deliver, to guide OD professionals and clients through the appreciative inquiry approach.

   __ **A.** True

   __ **B.** False

3. One way that OD practitioners can begin using the appreciative inquiry approach is by adding positively focused questions to their coaching, consulting, and facilitating.

   __ **A.** True

   __ **B.** False

4. What phase of the 4-D cycle includes developing statements such as, "We want to be the employer of choice," "We want to delight our customers," and "We want to envision ideas for growth"?

   __ **A.** Topic

   __ **B.** Discover

   __ **C.** Dream

   __ **D.** Design

5. In what phase of the 4-D cycle do participants explore and discuss their visions, hopes, ideas, and dreams for the future?

   __ **A.** Discover

   __ **B.** Dream

   __ **C.** Design

   __ **D.** Destiny

6. **An output of the design phase in the 4-D cycle includes powerful statements referred to as provocative propositions.**

    ___ **A.** True

    ___ **B.** False

7. **The 4-D cycle starts with dreams and ends with substantive changes in an organization's practices, processes, systems, and structures.**

    ___ **A.** True

    ___ **B.** False

8. **Although it is critical for teams to identify the desired future state when planning a change initiative, individuals can often design and develop the needed solutions.**

    ___ **A.** True

    ___ **B.** False

9. **What are the five steps in the Pfeiffer and Jones's experiential learning cycle?**

    ___ **A.** Topic selection, discover, dream, design, destiny

    ___ **B.** Experiencing, publishing, processing, generalizing, applying

    ___ **C.** Using questioning techniques, integrating multidisciplinary learning topics, using experiential activities to expand learning

    ___ **D.** Seeing, hearing, touching, tasting, smelling

10. **Which of the following is *not* a characteristic of experiential learning activities?**

    ___ **A.** They are directed toward a specific goal.

    ___ **B.** They are unstructured and free form.

    ___ **C.** They generate data and information for participant analysis.

    ___ **D.** They require processing or debriefing for maximum learning.

References

Biech, E. (2005). *Training for Dummies®*. Hoboken, NJ: Wiley Publishing.

Cooperrider, D., D. Whitney, and J. Stavros. (2003). *Appreciative Inquiry Handbook: The First in a Series of AI Workbooks for Leaders of Change*. Brunswick, OH: Lakeshore Communications.

Darraugh, B., editor. (1993). "Understanding Reengineering: Organizational Transformation." *Infoline* No. 259308.

Haneberg, L. (2005). *Organization Development Basics*. Alexandria, VA: ASTD.

Magruder Watkins, J., and B.J. Mohr. (2001). *Appreciative Inquiry: Change at the Speed of Imagination*. San Francisco: Jossey-Bass/Pfeiffer.

Pfeiffer, W., and J.E. Jones. (1975). *A Handbook of Structured Experiences for Human Relations Training*. Volumes 1–5. La Jolla, CA: University Associates.

Van Tiem, D., and J. Rosenzweig. (2006). "Appreciative Inquiry." *Infoline* No. 250601.

4
Action Learning

Action learning has quietly become one of the most powerful problem-solving—as well as team and organizational development—tools to be used all over the world. Companies as diverse as Exxon, General Electric, TRW, Motorola, General Motors, the U.S. Army, and British Airways use action learning to develop their leaders, identify strategic competitive advantages, reduce operating costs, and create performance management systems, and as a foundation for evolving into learning organizations.

Yet action learning is not used in most organizations. Why? Primarily because most people are unfamiliar with the basic procedures and capabilities of action learning. Secondly, some managers are unwilling to trust and delegate their power or control to action learning teams. And finally, some companies are not willing to provide the time that action learning groups may require to systematically and simultaneously solve current problems and learn how to handle future challenges.

Learning Objectives:

- ☑ Describe the six components of action learning.
- ☑ Explain how Bloom's Taxonomy can be applied to convey learning.
- ☑ Describe how Six Sigma processes can help transform an organization.
- ☑ Explain how the **Kepner-Tregoe** approach to change can identify needs and wants.
- ☑ Describe how action learning can be applied to group or team facilitation.
- ☑ Apply the action learning theory to meeting management.
- ☑ Understand how to apply action learning in a multicultural (global) environment.

Six Components of Action Learning

An action learning program derives its power and benefits from six interactive and interdependent components. The strength and success of action learning is built upon how well these elements are employed and reinforced.

1. Problem or Project

Action learning is built around a problem (be it a project, challenge, issue, or task), the resolution of which is of high importance to an individual, team, or organization. The problem should be significant, be within the responsibility of the team, and provide an opportunity for learning.

2. Action Learning Group

The core entity in action learning is the action learning group (also called a set or team). The group is composed of four to eight people who examine an organizational problem that has no easily identifiable solution. Ideally, the makeup of the group is diverse so as to maximize various perspectives and to obtain fresh viewpoints.

3. Emphasis on Careful Questioning and Listening

By concentrating on the right questions rather than the right answers, action learning focuses on what one does not know in addition to one's current knowledge. Action learning tackles problems through a process of first asking questions to clarify the exact nature of the problem, reflecting and identifying possible solutions, and only then taking action.

4. Resolution to Take Action

For action learning advocates, there is no real learning unless action is taken, for no one is ever sure the idea or plan will be effective until it has been implemented. Therefore, members of the action learning group must have the power to take action themselves or be ensured that their recommendations will be implemented (barring any significant change in the environment or the group's obvious lack of essential information). Action enhances learning because it provides a basis and anchor for the critical dimension of reflection.

5. Commitment to Learning

Solving an organizational problem provides an immediate, short-term benefit to the company. The greater, longer-term, multiplier benefit, however, is the learning gained by each group member and how the group's learning can be applied on a system-wide basis throughout the organization. The learning that occurs in action learning has greater value strategically for the organization than the immediate tactical advantage of early problem correction. In action learning, the learning is as important as the action. Action learning places equal emphasis on accomplishing the task and on the learning or development of individuals and organizations.

6. Learning Coach or Facilitator

Coaching is necessary for the group to focus on the important (i.e., the learnings) as well as the urgent (resolving the problem). The action learning coach helps the team members reflect both on what they are learning and how they are solving problems. Through a series of questions, the coach enables group members to reflect on how they listen, how they may have reframed the problem, how they are planning and working, and what assumptions may be shaping their beliefs and actions. The coaching role may be rotated among members of the group or may be a person assigned to that role throughout the duration of the group's existence.

Action Learning and Learning Organizations

Perhaps no tool is more effective in building a learning organization than action learning. Lex Dilworth (Marquardt 1997) has called action learning "the DNA of a learning organization," because action learning both enables and forces organizations to continually learn on an organization-wide basis and thereby be better able to adapt to the continually changing environment.

There are many elements of action learning that contribute to the building of a learning organization, because action learning

- is outcome-oriented
- is designed to systematically transfer knowledge throughout the organization
- enables people to learn by doing
- helps develop learning-how-to-learn skills
- encourages continuous learning
- creates a learning culture—learning becomes a way of life
- allows for mistakes and experimentation
- develops skills of critical reflection and reframing
- is a mechanism for developing learning skills and behavior
- demonstrates the benefits of organizational learning
- models working and learning simultaneously
- is problem-focused rather than hierarchically bound
- provides a network for sharing, supporting, giving feedback, and challenging assumptions

- develops the ability of members to generate information

- breaks down barriers among people and across traditional organizational boundaries

- helps an organization move from a culture of training (in which someone else determines and provides employee development) to a culture of learning (each person is responsible for continuous learning)

- applies learning to other parts of the organization as appropriate.

The next three sections cover Bloom's Taxonomy, Six Sigma processes, and the Kepner-Tregoe process—underpinnings of action learning.

Bloom's Taxonomy

Trainers often use knowledge, skills, and attitude—also known as KSAs—to describe the three types of learning.

These three categories are the work of Benjamin Bloom and are part of Bloom's taxonomy, a hierarchy ordering cognitive and affective outcomes starting with the simplest behavior to the most complex: knowledge, comprehension, application, analysis, synthesis, and evaluation.

These categories describe the ultimate goal of the training process—what learners should acquire as the result of training:

- *Knowledge:* Also known as cognitive outcomes, knowledge involves the development of intellectual skills. Examples of knowledge include understanding the principles of engineering, how to organize plants in a garden, or knowing the steps to complete a process at work.

- *Skills:* Also known as psychomotor outcomes, skills refer to physical movement, coordination, and the use of the motor-skills area. An example of skills includes the abilities to operate a piece of equipment.

- *Attitude:* Also known as affective outcomes, attitude refers to how a person deals with things emotionally, such as feelings, motivation, and enthusiasm. Although attitude is not taught, training may affect it. Although trainers cannot change attitudes, they can often influence them.

Each of these categories means that instructional developers and trainers may need to use different techniques and presentation methods to help convey the content being taught.

Six Sigma Processes

Action research assumes that the subjects of a research project and the researchers jointly contribute to the design and outcomes of the research initiative. The ***Six Sigma methodology***, the highly statistical quality improvement technique born in manufacturing bays at Motorola in the mid-1980s, is often used at an operational level to help cut costs, improve processes, and reduce business cycle times. Its value in that regard is well understood by business leaders. Strategic Six Sigma principles and practices can help companies formulate and integrate business strategies and missions; deal with constantly changing and increasingly complex customer requirements; drive revenue growth and systemic, sustained culture change; and enhance and condense the corporate learning cycle—the time it takes to translate market intelligence and competitive data into new business practices.

Six Sigma is a high-performing, data-driven approach to analyzing and solving root causes of business problems. It ties the outputs of a business directly to marketplace requirements. At the strategic or transformative level, the goal of Six Sigma is to align an organization to its marketplace and deliver real improvements and dollars to the bottom line. Companies such as Constellation Energy and Microsoft have successfully integrated action learning into their Six Sigma programs.

Kepner-Tregoe Process

In *The New Rational Manager*, Kepner and Tregoe (1981) describe a practical, straightforward decision-making process. First, they divide the criteria into musts and wants. The musts are definable into either-or categories. In a hypothetical example, one must might be for the vendors to have technical support sufficient to handle 120,000 registrations per month. The first round of analysis measures the vendors against this: Do they have this capacity? Those that do not are no longer considered.

The wants are those relative measures that are important but cannot be quantified into yes or no answers. Using the registration technology example again, perhaps the company wants to increase the quantity of training and education provided and is, therefore, looking for a supplier with a strong commitment to leading-edge technology that would enable it to keep pace with the company's projected growth. In such a case, the company would look for the vendor that shows this commitment more than the others. In such a situation, the team's assessment would be qualitative rather than binary. The question would become: Who is the best?

This is where a weighted comparison of suppliers can be useful (see table 4-1). Rate each supplier on a scale of 1 to 10 to determine how effectively the supplier met each of the want criteria. This tool provides a structure for identifying those wants that have the highest value and for weighting them accordingly. By giving careful consideration of the weights in relation to the company's goals for outsourcing, the team arrives at a numeric reflection of how well each vendor meets the outsourcing goals, rather than simply an objective but perhaps irrelevant evaluation of these vendors.

Table 4-1 has been expanded and filled in, and the next steps taken to create a weighted analysis of the company's wants. The suppliers that make it to this cut are those that have already passed the must screening. This tool helps to force healthy discussions about priorities and then to understand how well each supplier may be able to meet them.

Table 4-1. Weighted Comparison of Suppliers

Want Criteria	Priority Weight	Supplier A Score	Weight	Supplier B Score	Weight	Supplier C Score	Weight
Distance learning capability	10	8	80	7	70	10	100
Industry expertise	9	10	90	9	81	9	81
Implements in six months	8	10	80	7	56	8	64
Totals			250		207		245

The priority weights in the second column reflect that distance learning capability is the company's highest priority and six-month implementation the lowest. Suppliers A and C are very close, and both are preferable to supplier B.

As tidy as the information appears in such a format, however, the outsourcing decision process is neither entirely quantitative nor entirely linear. Once the critical information is gathered and analyzed, it is healthy to circle back and check on things that do not feel right. Instinct can be an important ally in the decision process. It is equally important, however, not to allow the whole process to be undermined or scuttled for the wrong reasons. Once the team has quantified the prospective vendors' capabilities, it has the basis for a tentative decision.

Action Learning Groups

Depending on the action learning problem, groups can be made up of individuals from across functions or departments. In some situations, groups include individuals from other organizations or professions, such as the company's suppliers or customers. Although many problems (developing a performance appraisal system or marketing strategy, for example) benefit from external, fresh perspectives and expertise, certain problems are perhaps best handled only with people internal to the organization (for example, handling a morale issue or combining two departments).

Though a diverse group, members should be near the same level of perceived competence so they feel comfortable challenging one another. The group dynamics and the diversity of its participants are the keys to success of the action learning set. The group, sometimes referred to as "fellows in opportunity" or "comrades in adversity," should include people who care about the problem, know something about the problem, and have the power to carry out the recommendations of the group. Although the action learning group may occasionally call on external experts and specialists when desired, these experts should not be thrust upon the group.

The group plays many roles for the client (who may be the organization or the individual with the project or problem). Groups can be a support network, a resource for information and ideas, a problem-solving forum, or a sympathetic, constructive challenger. To be effective, the group members should possess

- dedication to solving the problem

- ability to listen and to question self and others

- willingness to be open and learn from other group members

- value and respect for others

- dedication to taking action and achieving success

- awareness of their own and others' ability to learn and develop.

Selection of Action Learning Projects or Tasks

One of the fundamental beliefs of action learning is that adults learn best when undertaking action, which they then reflect on and learn from. A project or task gives the group something to focus on that is real and important, something that is relevant and important to them. It creates a hook on which to test stored-up knowledge.

There are several criteria for determining if the project is appropriate for an action learning group: reality, feasibility, authority, and learning opportunities.

Reality

The project chosen by or for the group must be a real organizational problem, task, or issue that needs to be addressed. It exists in a real-time frame, such as how to adapt to a new culture or decrease time between design and production. The problem should be of genuine significance to the company. This rules out projects or tasks that are created to give trainees a realistic problem. Additionally, the organization should expect a tangible result by a definite date so as to justify the investment of time and funds.

Feasibility

The project must be feasible; that is, within the competence of the group. For example, a group with no financial or legal knowledge should not work on those issues.

Authority

The task or issue should be within the group's sphere of responsibility, or the group should be given the authority to do something about the problem, such as including their recommendations in future employee orientation programs.

Learning Opportunities

The project should provide learning opportunities for members. It should also have possible applications to other parts of the organization, such as marketing strategies developed for one product that can be applied to other products or group dynamics that can be applied to other groups within the organization.

Questioning and Reflection Process

Action learning focuses on what people don't know as well as what they do know by asking questions that clarify a problem, identifying possible solutions, and then taking some type of action.

Action learning employs the formula $L=P+Q+R$, where learning (L) is equal to programmed instruction (P; knowledge in current use, books, the person's mind, organizational memory, and so on) plus questioning (Q; fresh insights into what is not yet known) plus reflection (R; recalling, thinking about, pulling apart, making sense, or trying to understand).

For example, L (discovering how to motivate employees during a downsizing) is equal to P (book knowledge, experience, expert advice, and others' experiences) plus Q (reasons for downsizing, how to most effectively work with employees, and skills in communicating and motivating) plus R (reasons why group developed particular solutions and evaluations of whether solutions were creative, alternatives were considered, and effectiveness of the team).

Action learning builds upon the experience and knowledge of a group (the entering knowledge of the group is P), such as new concepts and ideas about downsizing, as well as its fresh questioning and reflective insights that can result in valuable, new learning for the organization and for the group.

P (knowledge) is traditionally used in most problem-solving activities. It allows for incremental, narrowly focused changes but rarely for sweeping improvements. If a person takes only presently existing knowledge about supervision (or marketing or productivity or training), but does not put it into the context of the day-to-day operations of the organization *and* his or her self-awareness about how well he or she performs, the person's growth and development (as well as the organization's) will be slow and built solely on external sources of knowledge.

Groups often have difficulty solving problems from a systems perspective. Q and R, however, are what make the real difference in the quality of problem solving and provide opportunities for individual, team, and organizational growth. Questioning and reflecting generates creativity, removes people from boxes, identifies connections, and develops systems perspectives. Typical problem-solving or quality circles focus more on symptoms because they do not get to the core—to the deep systems-based causes.

The major difference between asking questions in action learning and asking them in most other settings is that in action learning questions not only seek answers, but also seek to go deeper, to understand, to respond to what is being asked, and to give it thought. Questions are not a quest for solutions; they are an opportunity to explore.

Asking questions rather than immediately providing solutions unfreezes the group and defuses defensiveness. When someone gives advice or answers immediately to a person, it makes that individual defensive ("You must think I'm dumb not to have thought of that solution") or the group becomes boxed in (reaching a conclusion without having the context, the systems-based cause for this problem).

Questions open up the problem—they make it a group problem, not just an individual problem. Individuals are much more conducive to questions because they allow people to give answers and thereby have some knowledge and power that will be of value to eventually solving the problem. "You should have handled the problem this way" creates defensiveness much more than "Have you considered handling the problem this way?" The ability to ask the right questions when everything is uncertain and nobody knows what to do next is when out-of-box creativity emerges.

Helpful and challenging questions are essential to successful action learning groups. Asking questions causes people to think—provided they are asked in a supportive, sharing spirit. Helpful questions are those that get people to think more deeply, test their assumptions, and explore why they do things and what stops them.

What exactly are the helpful, right questions? The right questions are simply those that, when asked at the right time, supply the needed information. If the right questions for a given project are not asked, the information needed to solve the problem won't be supplied.

What questions do:

- Help clarify. ("Are you saying that?")
- Attempt to understand. ("Could you explain more?")
- Open up new avenues. ("Have you thought of. . . ?")
- Unpeel layers. ("And then what happened?")
- Offer ideas and insights. ("Would this help?")

Questions help unpack a statement and challenge as well as offer insights, ideas, and suggestions. During the beginning phases of an action learning set, six key questions are often asked. The first three questions can help identify underlying assumptions and expectations:

1. What is the organization (are we, are you) seeking to accomplish?
2. What is stopping the organization (us, you) from accomplishing it?
3. What can the organization (we, you) do about it?

The next three questions help the group focus on the realities of the situation:

4. Who knows what we are trying to do (who has the real facts and can put things into a proper perspective)?

5. Who cares about getting it implemented (who has a vested interest in getting the problem solved as opposed to merely talking about it)?

6. Who can get it implemented (who has the power; who controls the resources that can make change happen)?

These six questions always lead to more questions and generally to even more discriminating questions. As each participant hears himself or herself respond to questions, certain inconsistencies may become apparent; alternatively, talking out loud can lead to people developing insight, ideas, or explanations that had not occurred to them while going over the issue in their own minds. The very act of talking aloud is often creative.

Moreover, it is not only the responder who benefits from the questioning process. As set members ask questions—and see themselves being seriously considered—it gives them confidence in themselves and their ability to ask effective and relevant questions, which, in turn, results in their beginning to behave differently at work.

Also, as group members are asked questions, they are pulled back or propelled forward into a higher level of reflective listening. This reflection is crucial to solving the problem and helping individuals and groups learn. It makes people more aware of themselves and what is happening around them. Action learning programs provide the essential time and space to stand back and reflect, to unfreeze thoughts, to rise above everyday problems, to bring things into perspective, and to listen so as to draw out the experience and practical judgment of the group members. This questioning-reflection process also encourages the viewing of each other as learning resources.

In action learning, members should be open to try out new ways of doing things, experiment, reflect on experiences, consider the results or effects of the experience, and repeat the cycle by trying out new knowledge in different situations.

The heart of action learning is the process of reflection. It is designed to develop questioning insight, or as Revans (1982) states, "the capacity to ask fresh questions in conditions of ignorance, risk, and confusion, when nobody knows what to do next."

Commitment to Action

Action learning requires action to be taken, not merely the presentation of recommendations. Implementation is part of the contract between the organization and the action learning group; thus the action learning formula can be expanded to $L=P+Q+R+I$, where I is implementation. After learning about supervision before entering the group, raising questions, and engaging in self-reflection, people decide to act differently after returning to their jobs. They supervise employees differently and see how effective a new method is, continuing to use that method if it worked and not using it again if it did not work well.

Action learning groups should have the expectation and responsibility of carrying out their ideas and recommendations. Merely preparing reports and recommendations for someone else to work out results in diminished commitment, effectiveness, and learning on the part of group members. Being required to implement, however, prevents the group from resembling a think tank or a debating group. As intellectually stimulating and emotionally venting as such groups might be, without implementation nothing actually changes.

Meeting Management

As a group effort, action learning requires collaboration, which means meetings. Skilled meeting management is a must for successful action learning. Excessive, nonvalue-adding meetings do not just waste time; they also waste the money of an organization. Meetings that become bogged down in conflict, veer wildly off topic, or involve people in side conversations or snoozing can cost the organization a lot, including

- estimated hourly salary of each participant
- estimated hourly cost of benefits for participants (usually about 33 percent of annual salaries)
- hourly cost to use facilities
- hourly cost to use equipment.

Multiplied by the number of hours spent in the meeting and the frequency of the meeting, this type of ongoing event can result in an enormous annual cost to an organization.

However, meetings do not have to be a waste of time and money. Meetings go awry because leaders and participants do not have the skills and knowledge to take advantage of meetings as a precious tool. The value of meetings lies in their power to generate excitement, creativity, and innovation, and the opportunity to turn a multiplicity of talents toward solving a problem or making big things happen.

The belief that great results will come of putting a group of talented people together in a room is incorrect. Skills and knowledge are needed to run an effective meeting. Making the most of the workday—including meetings—means turning ineffective meetings into productive, exciting events in which every participant can shine. This section outlines a simple, three-step process to eliminate unproductive meetings and to get more value out of meetings. The steps are

1. Get ready to meet.
2. Meet.
3. Follow up.

Obvious? Self-explanatory? Maybe, but most people go straight to step 2 and rarely reach step 3. All three are critical steps for holding effective meetings.

Step 1. Get Ready to Meet

Preparation—as in so many other areas—is critical for making meetings successful and productive. The urge to jump in unprepared should be resisted.

To prepare for a meaningful, valuable meeting:

- Determine if having a meeting is necessary. This means determining what the meeting is supposed to accomplish.

- Identify who needs to be there and what participants need to do.

- Prepare an agenda.

- Identify any tools needed.

- Invite the participants, and let them know when, where, and why. Distribute the agenda, and let them know what, if anything, they need to do to prepare. (Effective meetings also require prepared participants.)

After the participants are identified, it is important to determine what each person's responsibilities for the meeting will be. Is someone needed to provide specific background information? Should someone else come prepared with suggestions and ideas for discussion? Do the participants simply need to read a report and be able to discuss it intelligently?

It should also be determined whether everyone should be there for the duration of the meeting or if someone can simply come for part of it. For example, someone may only need to give a brief presentation of information and then leave. Another type of responsibility that may be required of participants is for them to play specific meeting roles, such as timekeeper, facilitator, or note taker.

Whatever is asked of participants, the meeting organizer should make sure that they are given a sufficient amount of time to prepare. Many times participants find that they have information that would have been relevant to the meeting but weren't asked to bring it.

The next step in preparing for a meeting is to create the agenda. These are some components of a sample agenda:

- *Meeting objective(s):* In calling the meeting, the organizer probably already has an objective in mind. The objective can be evaluated by thinking SMART: Is it specific, measurable, achievable, realistic, and timely? What meeting outcomes would indicate that the meeting's objective has been achieved?

- *Logistics:* The logistics heading in the meeting agenda indicates date, time, and location. When planning the meeting, the organizer should consider organizational priorities and events. Is this a good time to start new initiatives or add to people's workloads?

- *Participants and responsibilities:* Names of participants should be put on the agenda with an indication of what they need to do to prepare for the meeting and what responsibilities they will have during the meeting. It should also be indicated who will play the roles of timekeeper, facilitator, and note taker, so that these individuals are ready to carry out these functions when the time comes.

- *Meeting outline:* The meeting outline lists the activities that will take place during the meeting. When preparing the outline, the organizer should make sure to not cover too much territory. Keeping the activities focused on achieving the objective and prioritizing the activites in terms of importance is essential to productivity. Also, the organizer should include the amount of time for each agenda item to keep the meeting on track.

Once the meeting agenda is prepared, the organizer can identify the needed tools, such as

- audiovisual equipment
- a laptop computer
- an overhead projector
- whiteboards
- flipcharts and markers.

When everything is planned—including what the meeting is going to accomplish, who should be there, and where it's going to be—it's time to send out the meeting announcement. The announcement should contain the

- names of all meeting participants
- meeting organizer's name and phone number
- meeting date
- starting and ending times
- meeting location
- meeting objective(s)
- preparation required by participants
- additional materials for participants to bring.

The announcement should be sent far enough in advance for participants to be able to clear time on their calendars for the meeting and carry out any preparations.

Step 2. Meet

A hallmark of an effective meeting is excellent preparation, and that goes for every component, from the agenda to room setup. The organizer should get to the meeting room early enough to make sure that

- the seating arrangements are set up properly
- the lighting is appropriate
- audiovisual equipment is working properly and the organizer knows how to use it
- the visual aids are arranged so that everyone can see them

- all of the materials are on hand: handouts for everyone, extra copies of the agenda, markers for the flipcharts, and so forth.

The organizer can set the right tone for the entire meeting by

- starting on time
- introducing everyone
- explaining the reasons for the meeting
- forecasting the process
- explaining the ground rules
- displaying enthusiasm.

Now that meeting participants know what they are doing there and are excited to contribute to effective meeting outcomes, the organizer should keep the meeting running productively. To make the most of the time, the organizer should

- run various meeting activities
- communicate effectively
- keep the meeting on track (topic and time)
- manage conflict
- listen actively.

The effectiveness of a meeting is also affected by how well the meeting ends. The following steps wrap up a productive meeting:

- *Summarize:* At the end of the meeting, take a few minutes to summarize and review what was covered in the meeting. Go over the agenda points, indicate what was covered and what wasn't covered, and identify possible items for another meeting.

- *Open up the room for questions:* Allow at least five minutes for a question-and-answer session after the meeting summary to ensure that everyone has the same perception of the meeting and there are no points of confusion.

- *Gain agreements and commitments from all participants:* The meeting should end with all participants agreeing on the contents and outcome of the meeting. In addition, each person should have made a commitment to further action. Make sure that all participants are able to state what they are going to do and when. Plan to follow up at a later date.

- *Evaluate the meeting:* Periodically distribute an evaluation form to maintain and improve meeting quality.

- *End on time (or early):* Respect the participants' time and end the meeting as stated on the agenda. If some agenda points weren't met, plan to have another meeting. Always thank the participants for their time and participation.

Step 3. Follow Up

The organizer needs to follow up on the meeting:

- Compile and distribute the notes from the meeting. Make sure that everyone who attended the meeting gets a copy as well as anyone who is affected by the outcomes of the meeting but didn't attend.

- Follow up on commitments.

- Plan for a follow-up meeting to make sure that commitments are being upheld and the purpose of the meeting is being achieved. Also, the follow-up meeting will point out if any new problems have surfaced that meeting participants need to solve.

- If an evaluation form was distributed, review the comments. Resolve to make improvements as needed.

Multicultural (Global) Groups

Many problems benefit from fresh perspectives and varied expertise. The diversity of the group is a key to the success of the action learning set. Organizations that are knowledgeable about intercultural communication will have an edge. Organizations must assess their own level of intercultural competence and take action to ensure that they address the issue. Cultural diversity training is one part of the action.

Three interlocking steps are necessary to create acceptance of diversity in the workplace, according to research done by Myers (1990), a communications consultant from Solana Beach, California. The three steps are

1. recognizing the effect of different cultures on the workplace

2. taking organizational responsibility

3. training individuals to develop interpersonal skills.

To encourage managers to recognize the effect of intercultural communication, Myers (1990) suggests that trainers make their organizations aware that

- other cultures may not adhere to mainstream American norms

- biases against unfamiliar behavior and practices often exist

- communication styles often lead to miscommunication and misinterpretation

- traditional American values often conflict with values of other cultures.

To encourage organizations to meet their responsibilities for improving intercultural communication, Myers (1990) suggests that training and human relations specialists

- provide management with a thorough needs assessment based on interviews with workers and other information available within the organization, working from facts and not opinions

- get feedback to management to gain support
- develop a plan containing basic concepts, new awareness, and possible changes and present the plan to management
- incorporate cultural sensitivity into ongoing activities, such as training, focus groups, culture-specific days, posters, and special exhibits.

To encourage the acceptance of individual responsibility for communication, trainers can help their organizations' employees develop interpersonal skills. Necessary skills include

- using active listening and feedback techniques
- testing the accuracy of inferences and assumptions
- learning to read different nonverbal behaviors
- learning about customs and values, both the mainstream's and others'
- finding commonalities.

Important individual qualities that can be encouraged include

- patience
- empathy
- trust
- tolerance for ambiguity
- a nonjudgmental outlook
- recognition of others as individuals and respect.

✓ Chapter 4 Knowledge Check

1. **An action learning team is a group of four to eight people who determine the appropriate solution to be implemented when organizations reengineer and go through change.**

   ___ **A.** True

   ___ **B.** False

2. **The key benefit of having members from different functional areas of the organization on the action learning team is to provide a multidisciplinary view and fresh perspectives and approaches.**

   ___ **A.** True

   ___ **B.** False

3. **The major difference between questions asked in action learning versus those asked in other settings is that, in action learning, questions**

   ___ **A.** Are always open-ended and posed to each individual to solve himself or herself

   ___ **B.** Not only seek answers but also help a group understand and think through the possibilities

   ___ **C.** Are brainstormed prior to the group session by individuals and then shared with the group to maintain anonymity

   ___ **D.** Are closed-ended to bring the group to consensus

4. **Bloom's taxonomy and knowledge, skills, and attitude categories are relevant to organizational change in that any training or learning solutions related to the change need to focus on what new knowledge or skills are required for individuals to successfully perform their jobs in the new environment.**

   ___ **A.** True

   ___ **B.** False

5. **Which of the following is defined as a data-driven approach to analyzing and solving root causes of business problems to help organizations formulate and integrate business strategies and missions and to deal with constantly changing and increasingly complex requirements?**

   ___ **A.** Storytelling

   ___ **B.** Action research

   ___ **C.** Kepner-Tregoe

   ___ **D.** Six Sigma

6. **Which of the following techniques is used to assist with a vendor selection process by dividing criteria into musts and wants categories and applying a weighted comparison to determine the best supplier?**

   __ A. Bloom's taxonomy

   __ B. Action learning

   ↘ C. Kepner-Tregoe

   __ D. Six Sigma

7. **After action learning occurs, the action learning formula is expanded to include an I, making it L=P+Q+R+I. What does the I stand for?**

   __ A. Inquisitiveness

   __ B. Investigation

   ↘ C. Implementation

   __ D. Indoctrination

8. **Which of the following is *not* a criterion for determining if a project is appropriate for an action learning group?**

   __ A. Reality

   __ B. Feasibility

   __ C. Authority

   ↘ D. Flexibility

9. **Of the following, which is *not* a step to wrap up a meeting?**

   __ A. Summarizing

   __ B. Opening up for questions

   ↘ C. Norming

   __ D. Evaluating

10. **A trainer is trying to make his class of managers aware of the effect that intercultural communication can have on the organization. Which of the following statements is considered a recognized effect that the trainer should convey?**

    ↘ A. Traditional American values often conflict with values of other cultures.

    __ B. Other cultures are not able to comprehend American culture.

    __ C. American values should only be recognized if the company is in America.

    __ D. Organizations are required to take action on the side of minority thought processes.

References

Albert, B. (1996). *Fat Free Meetings*. Princeton, NJ: Peterson's/Pacesetter.

Buckner, M. (1999). "Simulation and Role Play." *Infoline* No. 258412.

DeRose, G.J. (1999). *Outsourcing Training and Education*. Alexandria, VA: ASTD Press.

Estep, T. (2005). "Meetings That Work!" *Infoline* No. 250505.

Kepner, C.H., and B.B. Tregoe. (1981). *The New Rational Manager*. Princeton, NJ: Princeton Research Press.

Marquardt, M. (1997). "Action Learning." *Infoline* No. 259704.

———. (2004). *Optimizing the Power of Action Learning*. Palo Alto, CA: Davies-Black.

Myers, S. (1990). "Basics of Intercultural Communication." *Infoline* No. 259009. (Out of print.)

Revans, R. (1982). "What Is Action Learning?" *Journal of Management Development*, volume 1, number 3, pp. 64–75.

Smith, D., and J. Blakesell. (September 2002). "The New Strategic Six Sigma." *T+D*, pp. 45–52.

5
Systems, Culture, and Leadership in an Organizational Setting

Successful performance in any organization requires both awareness and expertise in the area of *organizational culture*. In its broadest sense, organizational culture is manifested through the day-to-day interactions of employees who are often globally dispersed. Few members of an organization work as an individual contributor; most must engage with others to work in a team environment. Contributing in these complex systems demands an awareness of formal and informal leaders, organizational maturity, employee motivation, and the forces of change on an organization.

Learning Objectives:

☑ Describe, compare, and give examples of the evolution of the industrial and postindustrial leadership models and their congruent organizational structures.

☑ Describe the basic goals of leadership within and across organizations.

☑ Compare and contrast leadership and management, and describe the nature of their complementary relationship.

☑ Describe and explain the effect of the forces of change on organizations, and explore how these forces are driving a shift in the nature and practice of leadership.

☑ Explain the importance of creating a learning culture in a knowledge-based organization.

☑ Describe internal factors that undermine or contribute to a learning culture.

☑ Describe the importance of being a learning partner who serves all levels of leadership in an organization through learning expertise, partnering, and leadership programs.

Leadership Within an Organizational Context

Successful leadership is important to organizational success. According to DDI's Global Leadership Forecast 2008, 75 percent of executives surveyed identified improving or leveraging talent as a top business priority, citing it most frequently out of a list of 14 challenges that world business leaders recognize as critical for success.

Over 13,000 leaders worldwide indicated that their leadership development offerings did not prepare them to lead their organizations for the future. In particular, when asked about the primary reason that leaders fail, they ranked a lack of leadership skills (such as facilitating change, building a team, coaching) and interpersonal skills (such as building relationships, networking, communication) at the top of the list.

The respondents to the Global Leadership Forecast survey listed the major shortfalls in today's leaders and in leadership development programs:

- There aren't enough opportunities on the job for leaders to learn what they need to know or practice.

- Leadership development programs do not use enough methods to teach skills and provide opportunities to practice the skills.

- Confidence in leaders is declining.

- Most of the world's leaders are not high quality.

- More than one-third of all leaders fail.

- Leaders lack basic skills.

- Quality of development programs has declined.

- Leadership development programs are poorly executed and send inconsistent messages.

- Managers don't know how to—or just don't—help their reports develop.

As Paul Hersey and Ken Blanchard note in *Management of Organizational Behavior* (1982), "the successful organization has one major attribute that sets it apart from unsuccessful organizations: dynamic and effective leadership."

Defining Leadership

So what exactly is leadership? Some define it as the art of motivating a group of people to achieve a common goal. Leaders, using personality and skills, inspire others to achieve goals and objectives. In particular, skilled leaders possess the ability to

- influence people and organizations

- provide direction and strategy for accomplishing goals and objectives

- inspire and motivate others to achieve the goals.

Leadership is a process by which a person influences others (followers) to accomplish an objective and directs the organization in a way that makes it more cohesive and coherent. Leaders carry out this process by applying their leadership attributes, such as beliefs, values, ethics, character, knowledge, and skills.

Although managers are responsible for managing, supervising, leading, and so on, and are granted the authority to accomplish certain tasks and objectives in the organization, this power does not necessarily make them leaders—rather, it simply makes them bosses. Leadership creates followers who want to achieve high goals, distinguishing it from management.

Some leadership theories purport that leaders are born. Other theories suggest that anyone can be trained to be a leader. No matter which theory you subscribe to, culture and leadership affect each other within an organization, each evolving and adapting over time.

Edgar Schein (2004) suggests that the culture in an organization is created by the actions of its leaders. When a culture becomes dysfunctional, leadership is needed to right the ship. To facilitate transformation in the organization and its culture, leaders must be able to perceive a problem and recognize the skills needed to influence the organization.

There are five basic goals of leadership:

1. To create a positive and effective atmosphere for communication
2. To develop and communicate a collective sense of vision
3. To inspire transforming/transformational change
4. To provide a sense of direction for the organization
5. To provide a conduit between the organization and the marketplace.

With leadership linked so closely to organizational success, what do workplace learning and performance (WLP) professionals need to know to effectively prepare their leaders, leadership development programs, and succession planning pipeline to meet the organizational challenges and goals in the future? WLP professionals should have a strong understanding of

- the evolution of leadership models
- forces of change on organizations
- the need for a learning culture in a knowledge-based organization
- factors that undermine and contribute to a learning culture.

The following sections describe each of these items in detail and relate how each is important to WLP professionals working with and developing an organization's leadership development programs.

Evolution of Organizational Structures

An organizational structure refers to the design of an organization, such as the division of product lines, market areas, functional responsibilities, and the reporting structure of these entities. Leaders within an organization determine the organizational structure for optimal effectiveness and to seek efficiencies in running operations.

How do leaders decide which organizational structure is best for an organization at a particular point in time? Some leaders settle on one organizational structure and maintain that same structure for years. Other leaders perceive that constantly changing external factors require them to redesign the organizational structure in response, prompting many "reorgs" and changing the structure, roles, and responsibilities of employees often. Still other leaders base the organizational structure on the strengths of individuals within the organization.

Historically, many different organizational structures have been used from tribal, agricultural, and family-business organizational structures to hierarchical and flatter organizations.

In today's business world, complex problems cannot be solved by one person in a top-down (hierarchical) organizational structure. Because of the forces of change on the organization and the complexity of the decisions, today's business leaders need partnership and collaboration to effectively lead their organizations. To be a strategic consultant and leader, WLP professionals should have a sound understanding of different types of organizational structures and leadership models, which provide them with a bird's-eye view of the dynamics involved in generating and sustaining an organization's culture and success.

Tribal, Agricultural, and Familial Organizational Structures

The first organizational structures (tribal, agricultural, and familial) developed out of necessity. As populations increased in developing cultures, so did the need for more resources such as food and security. These increased pressures on the culture led to social hierarchies. Different cultures and circumstances produced different kinds of responses to those pressures. Typically certain forms of chieftainship emerged followed gradually by a whole class or classes of people who had leadership roles.

Organizational structures developed during ancient times of hunters and tribes. Tribal organizations were often structured and led by royal and religious power structures. For example, tribal hierarchies often had the elders at the top representing the chiefs and the leadership of the community. Their principal role was to provide a source of authority and advice, ensuring an orderly and systematic performance according to the shared traditions of the community.

The agricultural revolution brought with it a transition from nomadic and hunter/gatherer societies to agriculture and settlement. Agricultural societies not only began domesticating plants and animals but also began transforming from small, mobile groups of hunter-gatherers into sedentary societies that could support larger populations, labor diversification, trading economies, centralized administrations and political structures, and hierarchical ideologies.

Similarly, think about the organizational structure for a family business. Typically the family members, trusted colleagues, cofounders, and friends are in the key leadership or management positions entrusted to make decisions that run the business.

In these structures, a strategic leader makes all key decisions. In particular, these structures are useful for small groups or entrepreneurial businesses as it enables the founder to control growth and development.

In more modern times, many organizations or departments within large organizations leverage one or more organizational structures (hierarchical, matrix, or flat/multi-directional), which can be plotted on the spectrum in figure 5-1 based on their characteristics and authority.

Figure 5-1. Organizational Spectrum

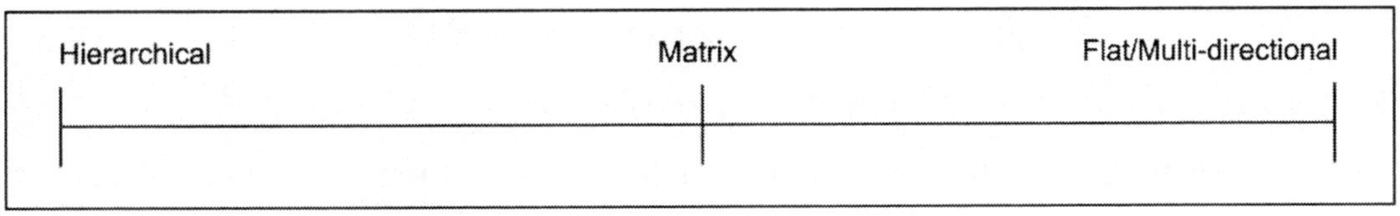

Hierarchical	Matrix	Flat/Multi-directional

Hierarchical Organizational Structures

The hierarchical or bureaucratic management structure (also known as silos or stove pipes) is used to create a strong, centralized organization with functional areas (marketing, sales, research, customer service, manufacturing, and so on) reporting to the CEO of the organization.

In this model, as depicted in figure 5-2, all activities are performed within functional groups led by a department head or a division head. Each department maintains a strong concentration of technical expertise. Functional managers can hire a wide variety of specialists and provide them with easily definable paths for career progression. The functional managers maintain and control their own budgets and the lines of authority and responsibility are clearly defined. This structure is often associated with industrial leadership models, which are discussed in the next section.

Advantages of a hierarchical organizational structure:

- simple and easy-to-comprehend structure
- well-defined management authority and job responsibility
- easier budgeting and cost control

Figure 5-2. Hierarchical Organizational Structure

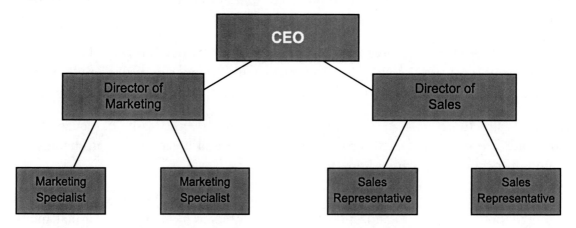

- better technical control because specialists can be grouped to share knowledge and responsibility
- good control over personnel because each employee has one clear boss
- vertical and well-established communication channels
- quick decision making within the functional area.

Disadvantages of a hierarchical organizational structure:

- little cross-organization communication from the worker bees to the upper management
- increasingly high-wage, low-skill frontline workforce with little chance of advancement
- ideas oriented with little regard for other functional areas or projects within the organization
- infrequent coordination among departments (or other functional areas) as department members are interested solely in their own internal operations.

Flat Management Models

Flat organizational models (also known as horizontal) refer to a structure with few or no levels of intervening management between staff and managers as shown in figure 5-3. The idea is that well-trained workers will be more productive when they are more directly involved in the decision-making process, rather than closely supervised by many layers of management.

This structure is generally possible only in smaller organizations or individual units within larger organizations. When it reaches a critical size, an organization can retain a streamlined structure but cannot keep a completely flat manager-to-staff relationship without affecting productivity. Certain financial responsibilities may also require a more conventional structure. Some theorize that flat organizations become more traditionally hierarchical when they become geared toward productivity.

Figure 5-3. Flat Organizational Structure

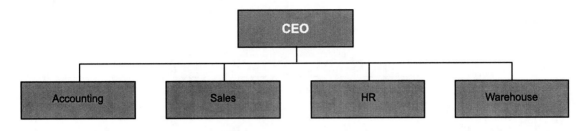

Some advantages of a *flat management model*:

- Employee involvement is promoted through a decentralized decision-making process.

- The level of responsibility of baseline employees is elevated, and layers of middle management are eliminated.

- Comments and feedback reach all personnel involved in decisions more quickly.

One disadvantage of a flat management model:

- Organizational structure generally depends upon a more personal relationship between workers and managers, so the structure can be more time consuming to build than a traditional bureaucratic or hierarchical model.

Matrix Management Models

The *matrix models* (sometimes called multidirectional structures) combine line and hierarchical structures with a general manager at the top of the hierarchy as shown in figure 5-4. The purpose of matrix structures is to integrate diverse areas of expertise. For example, projects in architectural firms often have teams of engineers, accountants, architects, computer analysts, and designers. Managers coordinate elements of their respective projects and gather needed support from various departments. Groups of individuals from each department cooperate with the project manager and fulfill project-related responsibilities. Department managers, however, have line authority over these groups. A challenge with matrix organizations is that there is often little to no loyalty of employees to the project because they are only on loan for the duration of the project. Their formal performance review manager (who also makes the hire, promotion, and fire decisions) is the department manager, not the project manager.

Large matrix organizations change constantly because the groups work as ad hoc committees, taking short-term assignments and beginning new ones when projects end.

Advantages of a matrix management model:

- Company can respond swiftly to client and project needs.

- There is no risk in losing the project in the bustle of company business because one general manager oversees all efforts.

Figure 5-4. Matrix Organizational Model

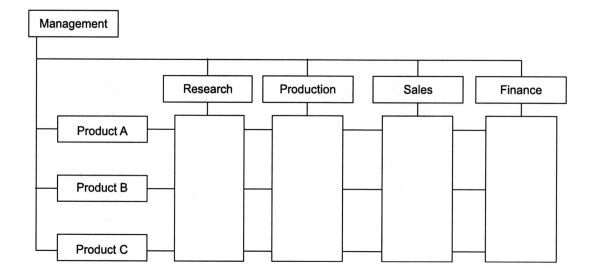

- Decision makers can take thorough advantage of the wide range of skills and specializations by applying these assets as needed from project to project.

- Limited resources can be leveraged across multiple projects.

Disadvantages of a matrix management model:

- Project and department managers can become involved in power struggles over getting project support and providing that assistance.

- This structure is more complex and, therefore, more expensive to develop and operate than others.

- A matrix involves a great deal of group decision making, which, if not managed carefully, can result in lengthy meetings and discussions.

- Power struggles often arise between individual contributors and their alliances to a direct manager and the project.

Fishnet

In *Upsizing the Individual in the Downsized Corporation: Managing in the Wake of Re-engineering, Globalization, and Overwhelming Technological Change* (1995), Johansen and Swigert explain that the "fishnet" organization is an alternative to the lumbering hierarchical organizations today. An example is the government bailout discussions of the Big Three automobile manufacturers in Detroit in 2008. These auto manufacturers have huge bureaucratic (hierarchical) organizations, which are slow to institute change and adapt when the business model needs to change. Many of today's corporate organizations are being built by people who believe in the rigid structures of industrial leadership models. However, in today's environment many organizational structures are giving way to more horizontal structures with complex yet flexible webs of interconnection.

During the 1990s many organizations began to take a different view regarding the structure of their workforce out of necessity. Fishnet structures emerged as an informal structure to meet the immediate demands of an organization and provide long-term flexibility. As shown in figure 5-5, the fishnet organization has a "visible form, like the strong rope or cord that holds the net together. But informal, ad hoc networks may then appear and disappear as the net is rearranged." The fishnet organization can only be facilitated by the use of information technologies, including a combination of telecommunications and computing. Information technology is considered the "cord out of which the organizational structure is woven."

The fishnet organizational structure allows the executive committee to exert control and continuity, while the decentralized units (where the work gets done) allow for flexibility in response to uncertainty or changes. One major difference between matrix and fishnet organizations is that the fishnet forms around the task, so the people accomplishing the tasks also own the project. There is no lending out of project resources as there is in a matrix organization.

The fishnet structure is flexible and "it can form and re-form varied patterns of connection. The middle manager may at one time be at the apex, at another in the middle. The fishnet organization rearranges itself quickly while retaining its inherent strength." Fishnet organizations have a dynamic flow of people around a problem, which enables nimbleness in response to internal and external pressures. Many people are uncomfortable with this type of organizational structure because there is no real structure as in a bureaucratic model.

Today, organizations are continually restructured to meet the demands imposed by the environment. Restructuring can produce a major change in the role of individuals in both formal and informal organizations. While these changes are well intended, many employees go through a process described as "freezing and unfreezing" during the changes.

Typically the employees resist changes unless they have compelling reasons to modify their behaviors and accept the changes. During this process—no matter which organizational structure is instituted—formal channels must be developed to ensure that each individual has a clear description of the work and his or her authority and responsibility within the new organizational structure.

Figure 5-5. Fishnet Organizational Model

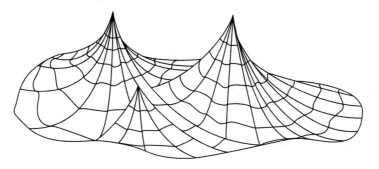

Understanding these various organizational structures and their implications is important for WLP professionals as these structures affect how learning is rolled out within an organization.

Evolution of Leadership Models

A review of the leadership literature reveals the evolution in leadership thought as a series of schools developed over time. Early theories tend to focus on the characteristics and behaviors of successful leaders, while later theories consider the role of followers and the contextual nature of leadership. Leadership models can be defined within two chronological time periods: the industrial and postindustrial.

Industrial Models

The industrial perspective of leadership is a natural outgrowth of the organizing principle of bureaucracy (the hierarchical organizational structure) and is congruent with Henri Fayol's administrative theory of management (i.e., plan, organize, command, control, and direct).

These ideas and models came into being during the rise of the industrial revolution when people were leaving their farms and moving to cities to work in factories producing tangible goods. Factories needed a way to organize workers with experience in a limited scope of tasks. Senior managers or factory owners led and commanded people to do their jobs in a certain way, and thus the industrial leadership model emerged. Industrial era leaders treated people as interchangeable parts, as easily replaceable as a part on a factory machine.

Industrial leadership theories made a giant leap forward following World War II. The United States emerged from the war as the mightiest industrial nation on Earth, winning the war in large part because of its ability to outproduce its enemies. Moreover, the rest of the industrialized world (i.e., Japan, England, Germany, and Western Europe) had been ravaged by war, leaving the United States as the only country still intact. At war's end, the United States shifted its wartime production machine into producing consumer goods, many of which were designed to rebuild war-torn nations. In effect, the United States had a monopoly on producing goods simply because other nations' production abilities had been devastated by war.

Almost immediately following the war in the early 1950s, business schools sprang up and began to teach business management and leadership. Researchers, scholars, and practitioners based their instruction of leadership and management on the modern factory as the epitome of how a business should run. The United States was creating great wealth, the baby boom was on, and millions of jobs were created and filled by willing workers returning from war.

Moreover, the United States was selling all of the goods and services it could produce. To that end, the industrial leadership models represent a hierarchical and frequently authoritarian perspective where leadership is vested in the most senior employees in the organization, such as the CEO or president.

In the industrial models, leadership is only what the leader does. Followers are simply expected to do what the leader tells them to do. James MacGregor Burns, the patriarch of leadership theory, succinctly explained this when he said, "the leadership approach tended often to be elitist—it projects a heroic figure on the background of drab, powerless masses."

Insofar as learning is concerned, the leader does all of the learning in industrial models. The leader has the supreme picture of the organization—often referred to as the vision—and the leader's job is to convince others of the worth of that vision.

One of the hallmarks of the industrial leadership theories are the mixed or interchangeable use of the terms *leadership* and *management*. The aphorism "If an organization is well managed, it is well led" fits well within the industrial leadership model.

Theory X

Effectively used participative management, a leadership strategy that had a tremendous effect on managers, was proposed by social psychologist Douglas McGregor in his thesis *The Human Side of Enterprise* (1960). The key concept is that leadership strategies are influenced by a leader's assumptions about human nature. As a result, McGregor summarized two contrasting sets of assumptions made by managers in industry.

Theory X, which is congruent with industrial leadership models, is the traditional way of looking at the workforce. Theory X is an approach that assumes that people would rather play than work. Theory X postulates:

- Most people do not like to work and will avoid it when they can.

- Most people need to be coerced, controlled, or threatened with punishment to persuade them to work.

- Most people want to be told what to do. They want to avoid responsibility.

The contrasting set of assumptions, known as ***Theory Y***, which is more in line with postindustrial leadership models, is discussed later in the chapter.

Great Man/Woman Theory

This theory assumes that leaders are born, not made. Essentially, great leaders will arise when there is a great need. Early research on leadership was based on people who were already great leaders. These people were often from aristocracy, as few people from lower classes had the opportunity to lead. This contributed to the notion that leadership had something to do with breeding.

Trait Theory

The Trait theory arose from the Great Man/Woman theory as a way of identifying the key characteristics of successful leaders. This theory assumes that people are born with inherited traits and some of these traits are particularly suited to leadership. Early research on leadership was based on the inheritance of such characteristics or traits. The underlying assumption is that if others could also be found with these traits, they too could become great leaders.

Group Approach

The group approach to understanding leadership began to dominate leadership literature in the 1940s. It assumes that leadership is the process by which an individual takes initiative to assist a group to move toward goal achievement in a given situation.

Contingency Theory

Although behavior theories may help managers develop particular leadership behaviors, they give little guidance as to what constitutes effective leadership in different situations. Contingency theory assumes that the leader's ability to lead is dependent upon various situational factors, including the leader's preferred style, the capabilities and behaviors of followers, and various other situational factors.

All industrial leadership models and theories blend the notions of leadership and management and essentially consider the two terms to have similar meanings. These leadership models also do not deal with the complexities of today's workplace and influential effects on the organization. Industrial models were solely focused on the leader.

Postindustrial Models

How do postindustrial leadership models differ? Postindustrial leadership models recognize that the level of complexity in today's work environment has increased dramatically, along with the speed of change, and the amount of information widely distributed to almost everyone in the organization. In this environment, it is everyone's job to learn continuously because leadership is demanded on every level of an organization.

The personal computer and the Internet have spawned a multitude of industries worth trillions of dollars. Technology has affected and revised just about every facet of work in the 21st century. Today we speak of the majority of workers not in terms of physical labor but in terms of knowledge work.

With the advent of knowledge workers and the role they now play in the economics of developed countries, there has been recognition of the importance of every individual in any organization to be a fully involved member of a leadership dynamic. Postindustrial models of leadership recognize this transformative change. They reflect the complexity of the environment within which leadership is affected and the need to meet the demands of rapid change through a transforming change process that seeks to invite followers, now referred to as collaborators or partners, to do leadership in the dynamic of an organization.

Leadership is no longer the inherent possession of only the leader. Further, in postindustrial leadership models, leadership and management have a clear distinction. Leadership is about making transforming change—creating greater levels of effectiveness—while management is about making incremental change, or achieving greater levels of efficiency. Organizations need both leadership and management because they are complementary processes and support each other.

In this environment, postindustrial leadership is incongruent with the structure and nature of bureaucracy because the factory model is entirely too limiting for the development of collaboration and continuous learning across the organization.

Theory Y

McGregor's (1960) Theory X was akin to the industrial leadership models. McGregor's Theory Y, which is more aligned with postindustrial leadership models, postulates the following:

- Most people will work to achieve goals to which they are committed, especially if rewards result from the achievement of those objectives.

- Most people can learn to accept—and even seek—responsibility.

Leadership in postindustrial times is defined by people working together to create transformative change in an environment built on trust.

Transformational Leadership

Transformational leadership is the ability to raise others to a higher level of morality. This leadership model assumes that people will follow a person who inspires them and supports the tenet that a person with vision and passion can achieve great things. Transformational leadership starts with the development of a vision, a view of the future that will excite and convert potential followers. Once the vision is crafted by the leader (or in collaboration with a senior team), the next step is to constantly sell the vision. This type of leader takes every opportunity and will use whatever works to convince others to climb on board the bandwagon. In creating followers, the transformational leader must be careful in creating trust as his or her personal integrity is a critical part of the package. In effect, the leaders are selling themselves as a part of the vision.

Collaborative Leadership

Collaborative leadership is characterized by very different roles and responsibilities. According to David Chrislip and Carl Larson, in *Collaborative Leadership* (1994), collaboration efforts cross many organizational boundaries. Because participants in groups come from different organizations and institutions, they need to work collaboratively to accomplish goals and objectives. Leaders can emerge in these situations that have no formal power or authority. Leadership in this situation is in what is perhaps the most difficult context, as all group members are peers. Collaborative leaders focus on promoting and safeguarding the collaborative process. They rely on the group to work with content and substance issues, while the leader's task is to ensure the process is constructive and produces results, not to impose his or her views on collective issues. Collaborative leadership allows for the talents of many to come together to focus on the issues and challenges at hand. It facilitates big changes as people define a future state and then work to achieve that change.

Servant Leadership

The servant leadership model emphasizes the leader's duty to serve his or her followers. Thus, leadership arises out of a desire to help others to achieve and improve rather than a desire to lead. There are two criteria of servant leadership: (1) the people who grow as individuals become wiser, more autonomous, and more likely themselves to become servants, and (2) the extent to which the leadership benefits those who are least advantaged in society.

Categorizing servant leadership is difficult. There is some debate as to whether it is an industrial or postindustrial model, and so it is a unique opportunity for WLP professionals to better understand the differences between the two leadership models. The dilemma stems from the use of the terms *leadership* and *leader*. This issue sheds light on one of the most important issues in the study of leadership.

Industrial models of leadership used the terms *leader* and *leadership* interchangeably. Industrial models are characterized by a few qualities: the leader does the leadership and the followers follow, the terms *manager* and *leader* are interchangeable, and the notion of leadership and management is hard to differentiate. The industrial models cloud the true difference between leadership and management from the postindustrial perspective.

Even though servant leadership extols the use of collaboration and development of followers, the servant leader is the single unitary actor performing acts of servant leadership. In line with industrial models, followers continue to follow even though they might be more inclined to work for or serve a servant leader.

However, in the postindustrial models, *leader* and *leadership* are understood to be two distinct ideas. The leader may be given the responsibility to deal with an issue, but leadership is the process of building relationships or other functions to transform a real, complex issue. More important, a true leadership dynamic involves a diversity of talent and the capabilities of others. The term *follower* is incongruent with the notion of a true leadership dynamic.

In postindustrial leadership models, the term *follower* is replaced with the term *collaborators* or *partners* because they are fully involved leadership participants. This is further clarified with the clear distinction between leadership (substantive or transforming change) and management (incremental change). In the postindustrial sense, leadership and management are different yet complementary processes that support the development and success of an agency or organization.

How then can a servant leader be considered a part of the postindustrial movement? If a servant leader sees himself or herself as the single actor in the dynamic, then it remains an industrial notion. In fact the definition of *servant leadership* centers on the leader as the main player on the stage.

If the servant leader sees himself or herself as doing collaborative leadership—a model where each stakeholder is co-equal in the process and where the functions or the process of doing leadership is focused on making transforming change—then it would make sense to include the servant leader in the postindustrial notions of leadership. To this end, the notion of a servant leader is postindustrial in its perspective, yet servant leadership remains industrial in its interpretation.

The industrial leadership models focus on the leader as a frontal figure who stands out as different and leads the rest of the people. Servant leadership theory now shifts the focus to recognize the importance of the leaders' relationship with his or her followers and stresses an interdependence of roles. The leader is now the team leader instead of the solo leader.

In summary, the postindustrial leadership models create relationships and partnerships to make transforming change within an organization. These models focus on the people and process of leadership. Postindustrial models recognize a clear line of demarcation between leadership and management.

Why is it important for WLP professionals to understand these various leadership models and theories? WLP professionals must be equipped to identify the models of leadership applied in their organizations and to effectively serve as strategic advisors to C-level executives by helping to choose or develop the right leadership programs to meet the needs of the organization.

Comparing Leadership to Management

Today there is a clear demarcation between leadership and management. Both of these roles complement each other, but the biggest difference is the type of change they work to create. Leadership concentrates on big, transformative, or substantive change. Consider the global financial crisis of 2008. The world's financial giants realized they could not continue on the same path, and experts stressed the need to transform the global financial mechanisms. This is big change that requires strong leadership.

Management comes into play once the global financial policies are changed or reworked, and the implementation of those policies needs to be completed efficiently. Management will tweak or create incremental change to the new policies to derive the optimum return from a given set of inputs.

Managers, by definition, have subordinates. Management is an official position of authority that focuses on carrying out the organizational goals in an efficient manner. Exceptions to this rule do happen in organizations, such as when a manager's title is honorary or is the result of seniority with no formal authority.

Managers have a position of authority vested in them by the company, and their subordinates work for them. Management is transactional—meaning, the manager tells subordinates what to do, and the subordinates do what they are told because they have been promised a reward (e.g., earning a salary or benefits) for doing so.

Leadership, although closely connected to management, is about influencing others (followers) in the organization to achieve greater effectiveness and fulfillment of the organizational purpose and goals. Leaders by definition do not have subordinates, at least not while they are leading. Many organizational leaders do have subordinates, but only because they are also managers. For example, the CEO of an organization is not only a leader, but also a manager of people with subordinates.

When leaders want to lead, they give up formal authoritarian control because following is always voluntary. Leaders often have a charismatic, transformational style that inspires others to follow. Leaders influence not only internal workers, but also external stakeholders such as stockholders. Leaders often perform an external scan; examine the strengths, threats, and weaknesses of the organization; and identify the gaps that exist and prevent the organization from achieving its goals. As a result of this external analysis, leaders build their strategic plans to close the identified gaps.

Leadership Styles

Leadership styles are not independent from leadership theories; they are the theories in practice. Leadership styles are the manner and approach of providing direction, implementing plans, and motivating people.

There are as many different leadership styles as there are leaders. The following classification of leadership styles can help WLP professionals to recognize not only the various leadership styles within an organization but also their own leadership styles. This enables WLP professionals to adapt their own styles as needed.

The Contingency leadership theory assumes that the leader's ability to lead is dependent upon various situational factors, including the leader's preferred style, the capabilities and behaviors of followers, and other situational factors. Leaders employ different styles of leadership depending on the needs and skills of employees as well as workplace constraints and circumstances.

Although the list of different leadership styles is vast, most of them fall into the following categories:

- *Directive leadership:* Specific advice is given to the group, and ground rules and structure are established. For example, clarifying expectations, specifying or assigning certain work tasks to be followed.

- *Supportive leadership:* Good relations are promoted with the group, and sensitivity to subordinates' needs is shown.

- *Participative leadership:* Decision making is based on consultation with the group, and information is shared with the group.

- *Achievement-oriented leadership:* Challenging goals are set and high performance is encouraged while confidence is shown in the group's ability.

No matter what role leaders and WLP professionals hold within an organization, the leadership style adopted is critical to their success. By understanding these leadership styles and their effect, WLP professionals can understand more about the leaders that they interact with and can develop themselves into more flexible, better leaders.

Forces of Change on Organizations

How many organizational changes have you experienced during your career? Think about how often some organizations change their structures, performance appraisal forms, leadership, or processes.

Many organizational change initiatives involve major role shifts and realignments of systems, processes, and culture. Leaders within organizations often need to drive change through the organization to accomplish the business goals and objectives.

To facilitate change, there are several driving forces required to shift industrial leadership models to the postindustrial perspective:

Speed of Change

The growth of content, innovation, and technology is faster now than any other era in history. This speed of innovation drives the speed of change in organizations. Keeping up with the rapid pace of change in today's world is essential for today's leaders and organizations to succeed. Peter Senge, author of *The Fifth Discipline* (2006), points out that leaders can't keep up with rapid change through the traditional top-down control mentalities, nor can they do it with no formal structure or processes, or total chaos would ensue. Today's leaders need to find the right balance between too much and too little structure for an organization to rapidly adapt its capabilities to survive.

Due to the seriousness of today's change-related problems and the great potential for opportunities, it is essential that as many people as possible learn how to better assimilate major change transitions. This challenge is best approached, however, by focusing on those in leadership positions. Only leaders—those who hold positions of formal and informal influence—can cast aside outdated methods of change and embrace new behaviors and procedures.

Information Overload of Knowledge Workers

In today's organizations, people are overwhelmed with information. For example, Ford has more than 300,000 IT users, in 20 basic business functions, interacting through more than 2,400 applications. The users of all of this technology can easily be overwhelmed. To move organizations to postindustrial models, people must be empowered to find solutions to problems because all decisions can't be pushed from the top down.

Complex Issues and Tasks

Change initiatives in an organization vary in size and scope. If the change is a simple one, known as incremental change, the organization is essentially asking people to continue what they are doing, but in a faster, better, cheaper way. If the change is more complex, but other organizations have undertaken this change and their best practices (or benchmarks) can help guide your organization's change, it is a transitional change. The most difficult type of change, known as transformational, will alter the course of things in the industry and put the organization on the forefront of a new paradigm. Depending on the type of change, there may be various external forces driving the change in the organization.

Global Competition and Globalization

Globalization in its literal sense is the transformational process of local or regional phenomena into global ones. It can be described as a process of blending or homogenization by which the people of the world are unified into a single society and function. This process is a combination of economic, technological, socio-cultural, and political forces. Globalization is often used to refer to economic globalization, which is the integration of national economies into the international economy through trade, foreign direct investment, capital flows, migration, and the spread of technology. The changing landscape of competition from across the sea often forces organizations to change to keep pace and continue to compete in the market.

When the economy became global, technology, which had been a competitive advantage only for a few big companies with deep pockets, became affordable and widely available. Competition forced organizations to make process improvements, operate with less overhead, and become more efficient.

Restructured Organizations

For organizations to work, several elements must align: structure, strategy, work and job designs, systems and processes, people, rewards, and culture. Each time organizations change any of these, there is a chance that the people and processes no longer align with the organization's business goals and objectives.

Increased Turnover

Succession planning is a systematic process for identifying and developing candidates to fill leadership or management positions. As senior and experienced workers leave an organization, a potential knowledge and skill gap exists unless the organization is proactively developing its talent to fill these gaps. Most organizations have no succession plan.

Lack of Training

In DDI's Global Leadership Forecast 2008, human resources (HR) professionals indicated that, on average, 37 percent of those who fill leadership positions fail. This trend indicates that leaders and managers are increasingly dissatisfied with their internal development programs. A business would not survive if over one-third of its customers were dissatisfied with its goods and services. Yet, most leaders and managers were not satisfied with what their organization offered to help them develop their own leadership capabilities. In fact, this most recent measure was at its lowest point since the survey data started in 2001.

When the respondents were asked about the primary reason that leaders fail, they ranked leadership skills and interpersonal skills (such as building relationships, networking, and communication) at the top of their list. Flaws in basic interpersonal skills were found at every organizational level.

Decreased Loyalty to Employers

Turnover can drive change in an organization. Today's workers have an amazing amount of skill and knowledge, and for many organizations these knowledge workers are the glue that continues to hold the organization and its processes together. With competitors offering better salaries, career advancement, and job security, today's employees are much less loyal to employers compared to previous generations.

Increased Demand for Employee Job Satisfaction

Today's employees are more likely to jump to different organizations during their careers to find more and more job satisfaction. The flux of incoming and outgoing people brings different perspectives and work experiences. It may take some employees time to adjust to the organizational culture and processes of the new employer.

Transferred Knowledge to Emerging Leaders

Leaders who move up the management ladder face special challenges as they make the transition from one level of responsibility to the next, often due to a lack of experienced midlevel managers to facilitate the process. A recent study ranked making a transition at work first in level of difficulty from a list of nine life challenges, outpacing events such as bereavement, divorce, and moving.

With each step up the corporate ladder, leaders' responsibilities expand and their decisions affect more people. Although emerging leaders and the transition process are a significant force of change within an organization, many have no development program for the transition to strategic leader. Even those organizations with transition preparation programs fell short as their leaders indicated that they still felt ill-equipped for their expanding roles.

Senior Leadership Hired Externally

When organizations hire externally for top leadership and management positions, the new leader/manager may have numerous benefits, and may serve as a force of change on the organization.

Executives from other companies or other industries bring with them fresh ideas and processes, particularly in key functional areas such as HR, finance, and supply chain management. A senior hire in one discipline will bring a wealth of ideas that can improve other parts of the organization. In addition to the acquisition of best practices, looking outside for talent helps an organization benchmark itself.

However, new leaders bring with them previous organizational structures and cultures that they may wish to change in the current organization.

Whether an external hire succeeds in the new position often depends on the company's HR team. The HR team should understand a company's business strategy and proactively put systems in place to ensure new executives adjust to their new culture. The HR department provides the new executive with a mentoring and coaching network that will serve as a guide through the critical first two months on the job. The executive should refrain from making radical changes at the start of his or her tenure.

Increased Diversity in the Workforce

Integrating diversity (such as different genders, ages, races, and cultures) into organizational change efforts can enhance the success of most types of organizational change. Organizational change and diversity efforts are linked; most organizational changes involve components of diversity. For example, an organizational redesign may combine functions that have previously been separate, such as marketing and manufacturing. The combination of these two cultures requires special attention to their similarities and differences.

One example of workplace diversity is the gap between generations in the workplace. The United States is undergoing the biggest generational transition in history. Approximately 77.5 million baby boomers will begin retiring in the next five years, and within the next 15 years, the workplace will shift to a new generation of leaders with an entirely different approach to leadership. The unique work ethics and values of each generation define the gap between the generations. For example, baby boomers are willing to sacrifice family time to climb the corporate ladder and reap bigger incomes, while members of Generation Y want challenging work assignments, but are not willing to sacrifice their personal lives. Embracing the differences and hiring all types of workers may ease the transition.

How does the generational gap and a diverse group of leaders affect today's work environment? WLP professionals need to understand what motivates each generational group and to provide learning opportunities that are flexible enough to meet the needs and interests of each group. Few organizations can afford to turn off this next generation of leaders.

Organizations will need to learn how to deal with external forces that are fundamentally reshaping its environment. Today's organizations face change forces from inside and outside of the organization. It is up to the leadership and the change leaders—the people who study models and practices for guiding change within organizations—to ensure that the desired changes are implemented successfully and that negative forces are minimized or eliminated.

The Need for a Learning Culture

Peter Senge is the creator of the "learning organization" philosophy, which he defines as an organization "where people continually expand their capacity to create the results they truly desire, where new and expansive patterns of thinking are nurtured, where collective aspiration is set free, and where people are continually learning how to learn together."

Organizations have seen the rise of the learning organization philosophy. The learning organization is one that promotes, encourages, and sets itself up to provide an environment built on the need for continuous learning.

In knowledge-based organizations, leaders should be focused on creating a leadership culture that promotes and values interdependence, adaptability, flexibility, and autonomy.

Senge notes that as the world becomes more interconnected and business becomes more complex and dynamic, work must become more "learningful." He also points out that organizations can no longer rely on any one person to learn for the organization and then have everyone else following the "orders of the grand strategist." In this respect, postindustrial leadership models and the learning organization are congruent concepts. The organizations that will survive and thrive in the future are those that tap into the worker's commitment and capacity to learn at all levels in the organization.

A cornerstone of the learning organization is personal mastery, where organizations encourage the growth of their people by supporting a commitment to development and lifelong learning. Senge postulates that organizations learn only through individuals who learn. Individual learning does not guarantee organizational learning, but no organizational learning occurs without individual learning.

Personal mastery is a process and a lifelong discipline. As such, organizations focus on the percentage of informal versus formal training. To support lifelong learning, knowledge workers learn through traditional training methods, but also through informal methods such as learning from co-workers, working in teams, and so on. In a learning organization, creating a learning culture is everyone's responsibility.

Defining a Learning Culture

Most organizations today realize that managing talent has the same importance as managing other aspects of performance, such as systems or processes. Companies feel the pressure to innovate and to continually energize their most important competitive advantage: their people. Peter Senge defines a learning organization as "an organization that is continually expanding its capacity to create its future." The term *learning organization* eventually arose as a convenient umbrella term to designate the kind of organization that commits itself to disciplines such as systems thinking, mental models, personal mastery, shared vision, and dialogue to develop its learning capabilities.

There are several factors that undermine a learning culture, as well as several factors that contribute to a learning culture.

Factors that Undermine a Learning Culture

A learning organization is an ideal. In one sense, all organizations that continue as the world around them changes are learning, but some are better at it than others. While these learning organizations are doing some things right, they still face internal factors that can undermine their progress toward a learning culture. Some of these internal challenges include competition for scarce resources, conflicting and competing goals among departments and groups, and lack of support.

Competition for Scarce Resources

In the global economy, organizations can look for talent around the world, but even those workers who may be plentiful and cheap now need to grow their skills. Companies in China and India, two fast-growing economies, are already finding that competition is high for scarce resources. In particular, these countries have already found that employees with a lack of managerial skills can hold back growth.

Conflicting and Competing Goals Among Departments and Groups

Departments or functional business lines have conflicting and competing goals. Every organization has limited resources to achieve the business goals and objectives. When different groups have competing goals, they are unwisely using up valuable company resources and hindering achievement of the organizational goals.

Lack of Support

In hierarchical organizational structures, where lines of business are operating in their own silos, a lack of communication and formal structures can undermine the development of a learning culture. For example, organizational boundaries prevent collaboration among colleagues, which prevents personal mastery, so the learning culture of the organization becomes stagnant. It is only when organizational boundaries between departments and groups are broken down that the organization can realize a culture of learning via collaboration.

Factors that Contribute to a Learning Culture

According to Peter Senge, the line manager has the most responsibility for employees' growth and development, not the HR department. The line manager must be committed to learning as an organization. A line manager in a learning-oriented organization is responsible for producing results and enhancing the capacity of people to produce results in the future. While the HR function can help this work, it is the learning environment in the day-to-day work that truly matters in growing people. Some additional factors that contribute to a learning culture are team building, reaching across departmental boundaries, participating in constructive conflict resolution, modeling organizational values and integrity, and promoting the learning culture through informal means.

Team Building

The capabilities of working teams determine what an organization can achieve. In *The Fifth Discipline* (2006), Senge asserts that the working team is the fundamental learning unit in any organization. The success of a team is never just a matter of adding up individual skills or learning. For example, one cannot just gather a group of excellent basketball players or a group of exceptional performing artists and expect to get good results. A team of any kind must grow and develop together.

Reaching Across Departmental Boundaries

As Senge notes, "Organizations learn only through individuals who learn. Individual learning does not guarantee organizational learning, but without it, no organizational learning occurs." To tap into the potential of people, employees need to be encouraged to reach across departmental and group boundaries to collaborate. It is through this continued quest for more information and knowledge that the continual learning process becomes part of an organization's culture.

Participating in Constructive Conflict Resolution

Learning cultures are fueled in an organization when conflict is resolved or negotiated in such a way that all parties are satisfied with the outcome. Learning cultures can not have a divisive mentality. By searching for solutions, the individuals and groups learn, which in turn spurs further learning and promotes change. If learning is a part of an organization's culture, the right decisions are advantageous to all groups and departments, which is a win for the organization as a whole.

Modeling Organizational Values and Integrity

The role of leaders contributes to a learning culture. Personal mastery—the discipline of continually clarifying and deepening personal vision, focusing energies, developing patience, and seeing reality objectively—is a key tenet of the learning organization. For an individual worker to realize personal mastery, he or she must have the support and encouragement of direct managers as well as top leadership. These leaders need to model the organizational values and integrity that they want to encourage in the organization.

Promoting the Learning Culture Through Informal Means

In any organization, a great deal of information is shared through informal means, such as talk around the water cooler. The role of the grapevine in office life can play a significant role in developing a learning culture. When trying to influence and facilitate organizational and cultural change in an organization, strategically selected champions can help to promote learning in the organization by working through informal networks and in collaboration with others.

An organization's problems are easy to articulate but often difficult to resolve. Many solutions rarely address the underlying systemic cause. Most people do not know how to identify or solve the root cause of a problem. It may be difficult to see the interrelationship of causes that have existed for many years, whereas the problems of today are very visible.

It takes organizational learning and team learning to identify and resolve the underlying systemic cause. Organizations that focus on creating the right formal structures, resources, and strategies to support the sharing and learning of organizational knowledge are on the right path to resolve these challenges. Organizations can facilitate these processes through the sharing of best practices, building competency models, and training employees.

Role of WLP Professionals in Leading Change

What exactly is the WLP professional's role in facilitating a learning culture and leading change? There are four key tenets that WLP professionals should consider:

1. Work to be a learning leader.

2. Act as a partner and learning expert at the executive level.

3. Serve leaders at all levels of the organization.

4. Develop leadership programs that transform the organization.

The learning function is where many organizations need to reconsider how to learn, grow, and adapt to future requirements. Learning is usually placed in the hands of the HR department and occurs in a traditional class setting. However, classes take learners out of their natural environment, which is why activities such as mentoring and coaching have received more attention in recent years.

Leaders and managers who participated in DDI's Global Leadership Forecast 2008 survey indicated overwhelmingly that there were not enough opportunities for them to learn on the job. Leaders are often dissatisfied with the leadership development methods and tools used by organizations. While knowledge or how-to advice from books or online sources can be very informative, these leaders indicated these methods did not have a lasting effect unless they were followed by opportunities to practice and use their newly acquired skills on the job.

In the DDI survey, more leaders gave high effectiveness ratings to learning activities that involved interacting with others, such as workshops or coaching. Leaders gave their highest ratings to activities that offered them opportunities to learn and apply their new skills on the job, such as moving to a new position or taking on special projects. For example, multinational leaders found assignments that placed them abroad the most useful.

How can the learning function break the current organizational boundaries to facilitate learning and change in the organization? WLP professionals need to partner with line managers. WLP professionals can examine the business strategy and the goals required to grow the business. In this role, they can help leaders and managers in growing their people. WLP professionals can augment and help to facilitate this process—but it must be managerial commitment and accountability to development people—not the sole responsibility of the learning function.

✓ Chapter 5 Knowledge Check

1. **A new leader in an organization is exemplifying all of the skills of a leader. Which of the following is *not* one of the skills of a leader?**

    __ **A.** Ability to influence people and organizations

    __ **B.** Provide direction and strategy for accomplishing goals and objectives

    ↘ **C.** Manage and direct the work of subordinates

    __ **D.** Inspire and motivate others to achieve goals

2. **A new executive in an organization has been using formal and informal channels of communication to inform employees about the values, beliefs, and vision for the future of the organization. By doing this, the executive is trying to do which of the following?**

    ↘ **A.** Apply leadership skills to influence others (followers) to accomplish an objective

    __ **B.** Apply managerial skills by directing

    __ **C.** Change the organizational structure from hierarchical to matrix

    __ **D.** Transform the organization from industrial to postindustrial

3. **Which of the following statements is a disadvantage of flat organizational structures?**

    __ **A.** Project and department managers can become involved in power struggles over getting project support and providing that assistance.

    __ **B.** This structure is more complex and, therefore, more expensive to develop and operate than others.

    ↘ **C.** The interaction among workers is more frequent, so this structure depends more on personal relationships between workers and managers. Therefore, the structure can be more time-consuming to build than a hierarchical model.

    __**D.** Struggles often arise due to the dichotomy of employees' alliance to their direct managers versus the project.

4. **A WLP professional is talking with a new senior leadership team to identify resources to support continued leadership development in their new roles. During these discussions, the WLP professional discovers that the leadership team believes most people need to be highly supervised and at times coerced to do a good job. Which of the following theories does this group subscribe to?**

   __ **A.** Theory X

   __ **B.** Theory Y

   __ **C.** Great Man/Woman theory

   __ **D.** Contingency theory

5. **A leader is reading about exceptional leaders in history and believes that these leaders were born with inherited traits suited for leadership. His thinking is most closely aligned with which leadership theory?**

   __ **A.** Great Man/Woman theory

   __ **B.** Trait theory

   __ **C.** Contingency theory

   __ **D.** Theory Y

6. **A key tenet of postindustrial leadership theory is**

   __ **A.** Today's organizations thrive on a top-down model of leadership.

   __ **B.** Today's organizations thrive by micromanaging the work of employees.

   __ **C.** It is everyone's job to learn continually because leadership is demanded at every level of the organization.

   __ **D.** The leader is the key person who needs to do all of the learning in the organization.

7. **In industrial leadership models, leadership was congruent with which of the following?**

   __ **A.** Hierarchies/bureaucracies with one leader at the top

   __ **B.** Collaborative and continuous learning of leaders and all employees

   __ **C.** Leveraging the dynamics of people working together to build trust and make transformational change

   __ **D.** Servant leadership where the leader serves the followers

8. **A WLP professional is researching leadership models focused on people and the process of leadership where there is a key demarcation between leadership and management. All of the following postindustrial leadership models support this distinction *except***

____ **A.** Transformational

____ **B.** Collaborative

____ **C.** Group

____ **D.** Servant

9. **A CEO often communicates the importance of "stretch goals," which are challenge goals that encourage employees and show confidence in their abilities to hit these goals. This CEO's leadership style is best described as**

____ **A.** Directive

____ **B.** Achievement-oriented

____ **C.** Participative

____ **D.** Supportive

10. **An organization is facing a major leadership deficit because approximately 30 percent of the senior managers are expected to retire over the next five years. When looking at potential leaders in the organization, the current senior leaders complain that younger employees do not have the same work ethic to be willing to work 12- to 14- hour days and come into the office on weekends. The force of change affecting the organization in this case is best described as**

____ **A.** Speed of change

____ **B.** Organizational restructuring

____ **C.** Global competition

____ **D.** Diversity in workforce across generations

11. **All of the following are internal factors that contribute to a learning culture in an organization *except***

____ **A.** A manager is most responsible for employees' growth and development

____ **B.** Building partnerships and reaching across organizational boundaries

____ **C.** Competing for scarce resources

____ **D.** Resolving conflicts and negotiating in favor of a win-win outcome

12. **In which organizational model does the line of authority flow from the top to the lower levels of the organization, and, on each level, managers have authority over their areas and subordinates, who, in turn, have authority over others? In this structure, every employee reports to a single immediate supervisor.**

    __ **A.** Hierarchical

    __ **B.** Matrix

    __ **C.** Flat

    __ **D.** Self-directed

13. **Which organizational structure's advantages include the following characteristics: the structure is simple and easy to comprehend, management authority and job responsibility is easily defined, and budgeting and cost controls are easier to manage?**

    __ **A.** Tribal

    __ **B.** Hierarchical

    __ **C.** Fishnet

    __ **D.** Matrix

References

Averett, P. (Spring 2001). "People: The Human Side of Technology." *The Journal for Quality and Participation*, pp. 34–37.

Bennis, W. (Spring 1999). "The Leadership Advantage." *Leader to Leader*, pp. 18–23.

Bruce, A. (2001). *Leaders—Start to Finish*. Alexandria, VA: ASTD Press.

Callahan, M., editor. (1985). "Business Basics." *Infoline* No. 258511. (Out of print.)

Chrislip, D., and C. Larson. (1994). *Collaborative Leadership*. San Francisco: Jossey-Bass.

Clark, D.R. (2004). "Concepts of Leadership." www.nwlink.com/~donclark/leader/leadcon.html.

Conner, D.R. (1992). *Managing at the Speed of Change*. New York: Villard Books. (Out of print.)

Darraugh, B., editor. (1991). "How to Motivate Employees." *Infoline* No. 259108.

DeLisi, P.S. (Fall 1990). "Lessons From the Steel Axe: Culture, Technology, and Organizational Change." *Sloan Management Review*, pp. 83–93.

Gilburg, D. (January 2007). "Generation X: Stepping Up to the Leadership Plate." www.cio.com/article/28475/generation_X_stepping_up_to_the_leadership_plate.

Harris, J., and S. Hartman. (2002). *Organizational Behavior*. Binghamton, NY: Best Business Books.

Hersey, P., and K. Blanchard. (1982). *Management of Organizational Behavior* (4th edition). Englewood Cliffs, NJ: Prentice Hall.

Howard, A., and R. Wellins. (2009). "Global Leadership Forecast 2008/2009." DDI Inc. www.ddiworld.com/thoughtleadership/globalleadershipforecast2008.asp.

Johansen, R., and R. Swigart. (1995). *Upsizing the Individual in the Downsized Corporation: Managing in the Wake of Reengineering, Globalization, and Overwhelming Technological Change*. Reading, MA: Addison-Wesley Publishing Company.

Kerzner, H. (1998). *Project Management: A Systems Approach for Planning, Scheduling, and Controlling* (6th edition). New York: Van Nostrand Reinhol.

Lapid-Bogda, G. (1998). "Diversity and Organizational Change." www.bogda.com/articles/DiversityandOrgChange.pdf.

Lauby, S. (2005). "Motivating Employees." *Infoline* No. 250510.

Maslow, A. (1954). *Motivation and Personality*. New York: Harper.

McGregor, D. (1960). *The Human Side of Enterprise*. New York: McGraw-Hill.

Mindtools.com. (2009). "Leadership Styles: Using the Right One for Your Situation." http://www.mindtools.com/pages/article/newLDR_84.htm.

Mische, M. (2001). *Strategic Renewal*. Upper Saddle River, NJ: Prentice-Hall.

Moss Kanter, R. (1985). *The Change Masters: Innovation and Entrepreneurship in the American Corporation.* New York: Simon & Schuster.

Murrell, K. (1993). "Organizational Culture." *Infoline* No. 259304.

Myers, S. (1990). "Basics of Intercultural Communication." *Infoline* No. 259009. (Out of print.)

Phillips, J.J., editor. (1997). *In Action: Leading Organizational Change.* Alexandria, VA: ASTD Press.

Quick, T.L. (1985). *The Manager's Motivation Desk Book.* New York: John Wiley & Sons.

Rose, E., and S. Buckley. (1999). *Self-Directed Work Teams.* Alexandria, VA: ASTD Press.

Rost, J. (1993). *Leadership for the Twenty-First Century.* Westport, CT: Praeger.

Rush, H.M.F. (1996). "The Behavioral Sciences." *The ASTD Training and Development Handbook* (4th edition), R.L. Craig, editor. New York: McGraw-Hill.

Schein, E.H. (2004). *Organizational Culture and Leadership* (3rd edition). San Francisco: Jossey-Bass.

Senge, P.M. (Fall 2000). "Lessons for Change Leaders." *Leader to Leader*, pp. 21–27.

———. (2006). *The Fifth Discipline: The Art & Practice of the Learning Organization.* New York: Currency/Doubleday.

Smith, W. (1989). "Managing Change: Implementation Skills." *Infoline* No. 258910. (Out of print.)

Straker, D. (2008a). "Leadership Theories." www.changingminds.org/disciplines /leadership/theories/leadership_theories.htm.

———. (2008b). "Leadership vs. Management." www.changingminds.org/disciplines /leadership/articles/manager_leader.htm.

———. (2008c). "Servant Leadership." www.changingminds.org/disciplines/leadership /styles/servant_leadership.htm.

Trice, H., and J. Beyer. (1993). *The Cultures of Work Organizations.* Englewood Cliffs, NJ: Prentice-Hall.

U.S. General Accounting Office. (February 1992). *Organizational Culture: Techniques Companies Use to Perpetuate or Change Beliefs and Values.* GAO/NSIAD-92-105. Washington, DC. http:161.203.16.4/d31t10/146086.pdf.

Van Wagner, K. (2009). "Lewin's Leadership Styles." http://psychology.about.com/od /leadership/a/leadstyles.htm.

Weisbord, M. (1987). *Productive Workplaces.* San Francisco: Jossey-Bass.

Wikipedia contributors. (2009a). "Flat Organization." http://en.wikipedia.org/wiki/Flat _organization.

———. (2009b). "Globalization." http://en.wikipedia.org/wiki/Globalization.

———. (2009c). "Organizational structure." http://en.wikipedia.org/wiki/Organizational_structure.

———. (2009d). "Path-Goal Model." http://en.wikipedia.org/wiki/Path-goal_model.

Zaleznik, A. (January 2004). "Managers and Leaders: Are They Different?" *Harvard Business Review*, pp. 74–81.

6
Change Theory
and Change Models

Organizational change is a consistent part of an organization's culture for those that expect to retain or maintain a sustained competitive advantage. Understanding the theories of change is essential. Change helps organizations successfully navigate and facilitate growth. Selling change and its benefits to the organization begins at the top, and the learning organization is an essential component. Change agents operate at all levels of the organization. Listening to concerns is important, because organizational change is personal. Change agents help resolve objections to change and help encourage alignment. Effective project management skills are helpful when implementing change. This includes evaluating the success of the project against success measures and attaining key milestones.

Learning Objectives:

☑ Define the current state of an organization.

☑ Define the intended outcomes of a change initiative.

☑ Explain how to sell a change strategy.

☑ List and define the rules of planning for change.

☑ Describe the importance of analyzing stakeholders of a change initiative.

☑ Explain why it is important to consider cultural implications of change.

☑ Describe the significance of setting milestone evaluations.

☑ Explain how to introduce change in an organization.

☑ Describe best practices for overcoming resistance or complacency.

☑ Describe at least four reactions to change.

☑ List the activities involved in implementing change.

☑ Describe how to evaluate the effects of change.

Defining the Current State

As the marketplace becomes more sophisticated and demanding, organizations must constantly alter some aspect of their operation to remain competitive. But, before an organization can implement change, it must first identify its current state, what is lacking, and potential approaches for improvement. In 1958, psychologist Kurt Lewin classified change process into three stages: the present state, the transition state, and the desired state. The present state, or status quo, tends to continue for an indefinite period until disrupted by another force.

Usually, some pain point is the motivator for steering away from the status quo. Such factors include shrinking market share; increasing customer demands; or continuing inefficient, obsolete processes. Why would a person or group be willing to depart from the present state for a transition state of ambiguity and insecurity? Because the pain of maintaining the status quo is too great. A significant change will be accepted only if it is proven to those affected that the present way of doing things is more painful than the pain that accompanies transition. The pain of the present is the prime impetus for movement into the future.

Organizational change practitioners must conceive the broad, aerial strategy and break this strategy into specific actions that move the change forward. Although there is no magic elixir to ease organizational change, certain tactics can help manage the organization's change efforts.

Defining Intended Outcomes

The first step in implementing change is to establish specific, achievable outcomes, such as establishing performance metrics or targets. The ultimate success of this phase depends on the initial definition of the business or organizational need for change. A front-end analysis must be performed to identify business goals, determine what performance is critical to achieve those goals, determine which performance outcomes have significant gaps, and then determine the cause of those gaps.

Because it is important to start with determining the business goal, it's critical to establish organizational priorities. The business goal ideally should be quantitative and time bound, and it needs to be a legitimate focus of the business. Additionally, some may be convinced that something is the real business goal when they've really only stated a possible way to meet a goal. These are instances where the goal stated actually implies or assumes other targets.

One example is employee morale, a common issue for many organizations. Plenty of organizations do an organizational climate study, a culture audit, or an employee survey and discover that employee morale is low. Senior management is then mobilized to do something about the morale problem, and that's when someone usually gets called into the office of the vice president of human resources to find out that the new high-priority assignment is to improve company morale.

In most cases, organizations seeking to improve morale are usually trying to achieve something else. According to management's thinking, if morale improves, then maybe turnover will go down or perhaps a more positive atmosphere would improve customer service. In addition, seeking to improve morale is often an attempt to increase the quality and creativity of employees' work.

In short, many organizations may claim the goal is to improve morale but have other intentions and are guilty of assuming that morale is the key to that happening. However, what's tricky about these situations is that no one knows what the real goal is. Thus, an organization may pursue an improvement in morale without understanding that the real objective is something else. That is why so many organizations that get internal audits showing low morale are galvanized to do something; they assume that morale is responsible for producing some business result. Morale can play an important role in various business results, or it can prove to be mostly irrelevant in the outcomes the organization achieves. It's important not to confuse the means of achieving a goal (in this case, seeking to improve morale) with the goal itself (what management hopes to get as a result when morale improves).

Ideally, business goals are time bound and quantitative, but many legitimate organizational priorities fail that test. The key is to not only accept goals with numbers and dates, but also confirm that the goals as stated are truly goals of the business and that the organization is not deceiving itself about what the real objectives are.

Selling the Change Strategy

Working on the assumption that analyses and solution selection have already occurred, practitioners can also assume that the need for the change has already been determined. It is up to the change manager to present the need for change in a persuasive and convincing way. As people are generally reluctant to change, organizations are not likely to embrace change for reasons they do not find convincing.

One way to make a convincing argument is to review what was discovered in the analysis. Explain where the company is, where it needs to go, and why. Be sure to identify how market forces and customer demands are affecting the organization. One piece of information that can prove a powerful influence is explaining the consequences for the company if nothing changes and these performance gaps are not filled.

Because doing nothing is always an option, it is important to enable a full understanding of what maintaining the status quo will mean. This may be known as pain management, which means information about the change must lead others to believe that the price for the status quo is significantly higher than the price of change.

When explaining the gaps between where the company is and where it needs to be, honesty about the challenges the employees and the company will face is imperative. It is also important to explain how the gaps will be closed, in what order, and by whom. This process of moving toward the desired state is known as remedy selling. Operational goals and how success in achieving those goals will be measured must be clearly defined.

The change manager is responsible for identifying and securing organizational sponsorship, and the sponsor supports the project by committing necessary resources. This is one risk factor in the successful implementation of the plan. Employees will assess the seriousness of the project based on a number of criteria, including the strength of the commitment among those sponsoring the change. Assigning the proper amount of people, time, and money communicates management's seriousness about the need to change.

Planning for Change

Plans for change need to be developed to define measurable goals, outline the strategic success factors, detail the steps for implementation, and outline how commitment will be obtained from key decision makers. Transition planning might also involve creating new processes, writing job descriptions, and establishing performance expectations. An organization development (OD) practitioner must identify which cultural norms and patterns, decision-making processes, and political environments need to be changed. Transition planning may involve developing the ideal organizational design. This is a time of running interference with senior-level stakeholders, ensuring their commitment offline, and confirming that the resources are available. John Adams, an internal consultant, offers 12 rules for project management success (Scott 2000):

1. *Gain consensus:* Stakeholders and team members must agree to goals and expectations.

2. *Build an excellent team:* The team must get smart quickly and remain ambitious.

3. *Develop a comprehensive and viable plan:* Make sure changes get communicated to everyone.

4. *Make sure resources are available:* Line up the personnel, capital, and equipment to do the job and negotiate as needed.

5. *Have a realistic schedule:* The fastest way to lose credibility is to change the schedule without a good reason.

6. *Do not try to do more than is possible:* Scope is the depth and texture behind the goals.

7. *Remember that people count:* Projects are mostly about people.

8. *Establish and maintain formal support from managers and stakeholders:* Make the approval process a formal event.

9. *Be ready to change:* Be prepared to be surprised.

10. *Keep people informed:* Communicate, communicate, communicate!

11. *Try new things:* Think outside the box.

12. *Be the leader, as well as the manager:* Plan, track, control, guide, motivate, and support.

The following sections discuss the five stages of managing a change project.

Stage 1. Initiating

This stage stresses the development of a vision and establishes clear goals. Key individuals form the core change management team. In this phase, the change manager

- determines what needs to be accomplished
- defines the overall goal
- sets down general expectations of customers, management, and stakeholders
- outlines the general scope
- selects the initial team members.

Stage 2. Planning

Planning involves defining the resources needed to complete the change initiative, devising a schedule, and developing a budget. It also includes identifying objectives and describing means for achieving them. In this stage, the change manager

- refines the project scope
- establishes a balance among results, time, and resources
- lists tasks and activities that will achieve the goals of the project
- sequences activities in the most efficient manner
- develops a schedule and budget by assigning resources to activities
- gets the plan approved by the stakeholders.

Stage 3. Executing

The workplace learning and performance (WLP) professional coordinates and guides team members to get the work done according to the plan and keeps resources and people focused on priorities. In this stage, the change manager

- leads the team
- meets with team members
- communicates with stakeholders
- resolves problems as they arise
- secures the resources to carry out the plan.

Stage 4. Controlling

The change manager watches over the project, measuring progress and correcting deviations. He or she expects and responds to the unexpected and solves problems. In this stage, the change manager

- monitors deviations

- takes corrective actions

- receives and evaluates project changes from stakeholders and team members

- adapts resource levels as necessary

- changes (usually reduces) project scope

- returns to the planning stage to adjust goals and gain reapproval of stakeholders.

Stage 5. Closing

This is the time for celebration and reflection. The change manager ensures effective closure and acceptance of the final product. In this stage, the change manager

- acknowledges achievement and results

- shuts down and disbands the team

- learns from the project experience

- reviews the change initiative's processes and outcomes with team members and stakeholders

- writes a final report.

In most organizations, it is absolutely critical that top management be committed and understand the changes to be implemented. A change initiative's success or failure hinges on that support. Three things are essential—communication, communication, communication—to inform all those who will be affected by the change. To manage a large organizational change, the accountabilities of all levels of the organization and key functions or departments must be clear.

Analyzing Stakeholders

Organizations need specialists who are experts in specific areas and who know more about a topic than anyone else in the organization. Line managers use the expertise of these specialists to resolve difficult problems. Because facilitating organizational change is dynamic and complex, the efforts of the specialists must be coordinated through individuals who truly understand the big picture, including the business, processes, and performers. Truly managing the change involves anticipating and dealing with or responding to the emotional reactions of stakeholders. Identifying stakeholders that are appropriately placed within the organization is necessary to have the influence and credibility needed for success.

In cases where the change leader is not already in the leadership of the organization, a change leader should ideally report to upper management. Upper management provides the support needed for the strategic alignment of the change process with the organization's business model, purpose, and values. Managers can provide the breathing room needed by communicating reasonable expectations and help provide needed resources. This creates the time and opportunity needed to build the process, structure, and skills for achieving early wins.

Upper management must be educated on how the change will add value to the organization. This level of understanding is critical for managers to take a leadership role in developing purpose and the agenda and selecting team members.

Cultural Implications

People go through several stages of readiness before they can make a true commitment to change. In the first stage, people deny that they need to change. In the next stage, people engage only in contemplation. They see a need to improve and are willing to think about it, but they are ambivalent and tend to put off making a decision. Preparation is the focus of the third stage: The individual recognizes that a problem exists and that there are ways of dealing with it. Only at this third stage is the individual ready to sit down and make a specific, concrete plan. The fourth stage is when the person acts on the plan (Prochaska, Norcross, and DiClemente 1994).

Too often, change initiatives assume that everyone is at the third stage: motivated, committed, and ready to develop a plan of action. Others recognize that the participants need to be motivated, and they include exercises or inspirational lectures to help motivate them. Very few programs pause to assess whether the participants have entered the third stage of readiness before moving into the training phase. If the participants are not ready, the time, effort, and money spent on developing the change initiative are going to be wasted.

In general, the percentage of people motivated to change depends entirely on how the change is sold versus some innate lack of commitment. If a sense of urgency is created, the benefits of a change are explained, and individuals have an opportunity to influence the change outcomes, the percentage of those committed to change can be considerably higher.

Milestone Evaluations

It is hard to isolate the influence of specific activities, the amount of change or learning, or the outcomes. Current accounting methods only consider the costs in time and money and are unable to adequately measure the costs of low morale or poor teamwork. The intangible benefits of an intervention—employee satisfaction, learning, or ability to change—are harder to measure. The investment in human capital does not appear on the company balance sheet.

Yet, it is important to justify the business value of initiatives. A capital investment of several million dollars would not be approved without justification. To respond to this challenge, many emphasize measuring the bottom-line results through return-on-investment. Still, many critics believe that the current financial measures are inadequate, not only because they fail to measure the investment in intellectual capital, but also because they focus on the past and fail to provide adequate guidance for today and tomorrow.

The achievement of milestones provides an opportunity to not only evaluate but also reflect on the learning and celebrate the contribution of team members and colleagues. A celebration lifts the spirits, reinforces important values, and provides a sense of accomplishment and closure for a successful project. Successful milestone celebrations

- have a theme tied to the purpose of the project
- recognize the uniqueness and personal contribution of the team members
- have a festive atmosphere with activities that are fun
- reward hard work, contributions, and accomplishments
- reinforce the values and goals of the project.

Introducing Change

In many organizations, the common wisdom is that resistance holds up progress and must be squashed or dismissed. Resistance is often not a response to the change itself but to the way in which the change or idea is introduced. The traditional, top-down coercion to implement a change forces employees to conform without any consideration of their concerns, wishes, or suggestions. Although the temptation is to squash resistance, organizations should work hard to understand its origins and address the causes. A discussion of the real reasons for the proposed approach and opportunity to contribute and participate usually converts the biggest resisters to champions.

Organizational change occurs only when the forces that promote it overcome those that resist it. People must recognize the need for change before they will accept it. Some forces that promote organizational change are

- competitive pressures
- legal and economic considerations, such as environmental and workplace regulations
- changing consumer desires and values
- cultural changes
- technological innovation, advances in telecommunications, and exponential growth in knowledge.

Change agents cannot control people's attitudes toward change, their levels of personal security, and the established organizational culture. They can and must, however, control how the change takes place (the rate of change). They must adapt their approach to an employee's current attitudes and to historical events, and they must work within the organizational culture's framework. Most people will resist anything that goes against the culture, so change agents must understand the existing culture as much as possible. They must provide the organization with a clear sense of future direction.

Overcoming Resistance

In planning how to deal with resistance, the change manager looks at a number of things. First, he or she assesses the organization's overall readiness for change and, based on the results, plans to lessen resistance. A *forcefield analysis* is one way to assess which forces within the organization will affect the attempt to introduce change.

Forcefield analysis, created by Kurt Lewin, recognizes two types of forces: driving and restraining. (See table 6-1.) Driving forces are those that help implement the change, whereas restraining forces are those that will get in the way of the change. Because forces are defined based on their positive or negative effect regarding the change, what may appear as a driving force might instead be a restraining force. For example, although incentive systems are generally regarded as a positive, if the existing system is not reinforcing the new behaviors, it becomes a restraining force.

The forcefield analysis ensures three things:

1. No areas have been overlooked.

2. The forces to be taken advantage of are known.

3. There's time to develop other strategies if the analysis reveals areas not considered previously.

Once the driving and restraining forces are known, strategies can be developed to either take advantage of drivers or reduce the effect of restrainers. By increasing driving forces or reducing restraining forces, the current status quo is moved in the direction of the wanted change. Because systems move toward equilibrium, it's advantageous to reduce restraining forces rather than increasing driving forces because an increase in driving forces also results in an increase in restraining forces.

The plan for reducing resistance must take into account the time necessary for both the people and the organization to react to the change. It must also acknowledge the reality that, although there is a need to allow time for adjustment, there is still work that needs to be done.

Table 6-1. Lewin's Forcefield Analysis

Driving Forces	Restraining Forces
• People	• People
• Economic benefits	• Traditions
• Environmental factors	• Organizational politics
• Employee needs and desires	• Employee attitudes
• Availability of technology	• Costs

Reactions to Change

An organization's need for change often conflicts with its employees' needs to maintain their sense of personal security, and change agents must recognize this. When a change is first introduced, what is the first instinctive reaction? It's survival, or how the change will affect each person. When implementing any changes in an organization, change agents must be aware of the effects of this natural conflict: the need for the organization to change to survive, and the need for the employee to maintain his or her sense of personal security. Balancing these conflicting interests may seem like an impossible task, but it is simplified if a carefully planned process is followed to manage the change.

Organizations are generally very diligent about managing technological change. Operating manuals and training sessions focus on the physical aspects of the change, and they are both routine and rigorous. Companies, however, do not pay as much attention to the psychological and social effects of organizational change. Psychological considerations include those that affect the way people relate to and feel about their jobs. Any change may create doubts and questions in a person's mind. The severity of those doubts depends partially on an individual's personality and experience. Many concerns, however, are predictable. Social considerations include changes in the individual's relationships with others in the work group and with the whole organization. Concerns include alienation from fellow employees, less access to information, and status in a new peer group.

Change agents focus a lot of attention on the behavioral effects of change, but psychological and social aspects are more important. Psychological and social effects prompt predictable questions from the people affected. Change agents should anticipate the questions and reactions that will arise from the change being implemented. The key lies in change agents placing themselves in the position of those whom the change affects.

An organization's people are a critical component in ensuring that any organizational change initiative is successful. Karl Albrecht described the personal change response cycle to help individuals work though the progressive psychological phases of change response. These phases are

- *Threat:* In this phase, individuals are afraid to change the status quo because of fear of the unknown or fear of a state worse than the status quo.

- *Problem:* At this point, individuals perceive change to be a lot of work and problems. Because they no longer know the rules, it's difficult for them to complete their jobs.

- *Solution:* Overcoming the problems perceived in the previous phase starts to reveal some of the benefits of the change.

- *Habit:* As old operating procedures are forgotten, the new become the norm.

Implementing Change

In implementing any kind of change, remember Murphy's Law: Anything that can go wrong will go wrong at the worst possible moment. Flexibility in implementation is critical. Change managers must adapt to cues and suggestions from the people with whom they are working.

The first cycle of implementing a change program can take from one to five years, depending on the scope of the change and the strength of internal barriers. Changing an organization that is deeply and culturally set in its ways poses a challenge for a change leader. Redirecting such an organization can sometimes take years of concerted effort. However, most companies do not have the luxury of waiting several years before they see the results of change. In today's fast-paced global economy, five months is more in line with expectations. This short timeline poses significant challenges, which can be overcome if the change is designed well.

Any major change effort comprises

- defining the tasks that need to be done
- creating management systems that accomplish the tasks
- developing strategies for gaining commitment
- developing communication strategies
- assigning resources, experts, and consultants to manage the change.

During the implementation phase, management must define what is to be done, how it is to be done, and who should do it. Tasks of a fundamental change effort include

- studying present conditions
- collecting data on employee attitudes toward the change
- creating models of the end state
- identifying and planning for transitional management
- assigning functions to transitional management
- stating the goals of the transition and clearly describing the end state.

Establishing support for change can be tricky, especially if middle and lower management and employees feel threatened by it. From the outset, a communications plan must be put in place that details the overall plans and a feedback mechanism that allows managers to know what staff attitudes are. Many organizations involve just the critical mass—the smallest number of people or groups who must be committed to the change for it to occur. Management also needs to determine the minimum level of commitment from key players who will allow the change to happen. This means deciding whether those key players must make it happen, help it happen by providing resources, or let it happen by not blocking it.

Monitoring for Compliance

An important aspect of any change initiative is making sure that the implementation meets the established objectives. At the outset of the initiative, regular monitoring cycles of the initiative should be instituted to ensure that it remains on track and complies with the goals of the initiative and is driving change toward the end state. Oftentimes, the implementation phase gets bogged down in specifics and details; therefore, established monitoring points will maintain the strategic direction.

Providing Feedback

The last part of the planning process is the creation of a feedback system that provides information regarding the results of the change plan. The purpose of this system is to provide information regarding the success or failure of the plan. This is done to design future plans that are more focused and better targeted to accomplishing a desired result. An OD practitioner should consider these important questions when developing a feedback system:

- What determines when the goals and objectives of the change initiative have been accomplished?

- Which type of early warning system can be created to inform stakeholders of impending problems?

- Which alternative plans can be created if the initial plan fails?

- How can practitioners avoid punishing people if the plan fails to accomplish the outcome?

- How will people be rewarded if goals and objectives are successfully achieved?

- How will the progress of the plan be monitored?

- Who will be in charge of periodically checking on the implementation?

- How will progress be measured?

- Is the feedback system comprehensive enough to successfully implement future change plans?

- Is the feedback system designed in such a way that it can be used in the design and development of future plans?

Coaching

Coaching is a powerful teaching and learning process that can enhance learning and effectiveness and help to achieve personal and organizational change. Coaching frequently is an integral part of the process of planning and implementing other initiatives, such as team development, survey feedback, organization and process redesign, strategic leadership, and large-group development activities. Coaching is defined as helping someone else expand and apply his or her skills, knowledge, and attitudes. It generally takes place within a defined context, such as a specific task, skill, or responsibility. The role of a coach might involve being a subject matter expert in a particular discipline. Or it could mean being a motivator whose pep talks and words of encouragement inspire others to greatness. It can also mean helping others set goals or find a direction for their efforts. Coaching might also be developing and maintaining an ongoing developmental relationship with one or more of the organization's rising stars. In general, a successful coach helps others succeed through guiding, teaching, motivating, and mentoring.

Evaluating Effects of Change

Evaluating a change initiative is important to determine its effectiveness. The evaluation process provides an opportunity to benchmark measurable business results and compare them with goals and results, as well as to find out what is and is not working. But how can practitioners arrive at useful measurements when evaluating the effects of a change initiative? One approach is to start at the end of the story, whether it is a certain job to be done or a corporate goal to be met, and work backward to develop performance criteria.

The most important thing is defining the key performance measures and identifying the right ones that are going to drive the organization to where it should be. To identify these elements, here are a few questions to be posed:

- What is the organization trying to accomplish?
- What does the organization want its employees to be able to do better?
- What are the baselines for measurement before and after the change initiative?
- What do employees need to know to fully implement the change?

Determining the right measures is difficult; however, it's a crucial first step in evaluating a change initiative. Once measures are identified, data can be collected and analyzed. When the analysis phase is complete, change agents can reevaluate the change initiative and make any needed adjustments for future efforts.

✓ Chapter 6 Knowledge Check

1. **According to Lewin, an organization must first identify what before it can change?**

   ___ **A.** Current state

   ___ **B.** Vision

   ___ **C.** Mission

   ___ **D.** Fiscal goals

2. **Intended outcomes of change initiatives are defined as specific, achievable outcomes, such as performance metrics or targets.**

   ___ **A.** True

   ___ **B.** False

3. **Which of the following is a strategy that WLP professionals can use to convince upper management that a change initiative is needed?**

   ___ **A.** Establishing performance metrics

   ___ **B.** Pain management

   ___ **C.** Remedy selling

   ___ **D.** Front-end analysis

4. **Which of the following is *not* a primary component to consider when planning for change?**

   ___ **A.** Gaining consensus

   ___ **B.** Conducting individual training needs assessments

   ___ **C.** Keeping resources informed

   ___ **D.** Developing an excellence team

5. **When analyzing the needs of stakeholders during an organizational change process, it is important not to allow individuals who specialize in specific areas of the organization to drive the process.**

   ___ **A.** True

   ___ **B.** False

6. A training program has been developed to help employees prepare for a new organizational process. While presenting the new course, a trainer sees that some employees are not engaged and sit quietly while others are challenging the details of the process. What is most likely occurring here?

   ___ **A.** The room conditions are likely affecting the success of the training.

   ___ **B.** The employees may not be motivated and committed to this change.

   ___ **C.** The employees have a problem with the trainer, and it is causing these reactions.

   ___ **D.** The training materials are negatively affecting the success of the training program.

7. The purpose of setting milestones is to provide an opportunity to evaluate progress and to reflect on the learning to celebrate the contribution of the team and peers.

   ___ **A.** True

   ___ **B.** False

8. What is the order of the five stages of managing a change process?

   ___ **A.** Initiating, planning, executing, controlling, and closing

   ___ **B.** Planning, initiating, controlling, executing, and closing

   ___ **C.** Controlling, initiating, planning, closing, and executing

   ___ **D.** Executing, controlling, planning, closing, and initiating

9. Which of the following analyses is used to identify driving and restraining forces and helps to overcome resistance and complacency in change initiatives?

   ___ **A.** Forcefield analysis

   ___ **B.** Cultural benchmarking

   ___ **C.** Cause-and-effect analysis

   ___ **D.** Five-why analysis

10. Employees go through stages of readiness before they are ready to make a true commitment to change. Which of the following best describes the second stage of readiness?

   ___ **A.** Employees recognize the need for change and create a specific, concrete plan.

   ___ **B.** Employees participate in needs-analysis observations to identify the knowledge and skills required to support the change initiative.

   ___ **C.** Employees deny the need for change.

   ___ **D.** Employees see a need to change but only engage in contemplation and are willing to think about it but put off making a decision.

11. According to Albrecht's change response cycle, when an organizational change is first introduced, which of the following response phases describes employees' initial reaction to the change?

   __ **A.** Problem

   __ **B.** Threat

   __ **C.** Habit

   __ **D.** Solution

12. Which of the following is *not* a phase in Albrecht's change response cycle?

   __ **A.** Problem

   __ **B.** Threat

   __ **C.** Complacency

   __ **D.** Solution

13. During an implementation process, a training director is tasked with developing a program to help employees through the change and provide them the needed information to succeed through development of new skills, new knowledge, and even new attitudes toward the change initiative. What process best describes what the training director is providing?

   __ **A.** Monitoring

   __ **B.** Coaching

   __ **C.** Providing feedback

   __ **D.** Evaluating

References

Cadzow, L., and P. Lake. (2002). "Drive Change With Case Studies." *Infoline* No. 250211.

Cheney, S. (1998). "Benchmarking." *Infoline* No. 259801.

Conner, D.R. (1992). *Managing at the Speed of Change*. New York: Villard Books.

Cowan, S.L. (1999). "Change Management." *Infoline* No. 259904.

Darraugh, B., editor. (1993). "Understanding Reengineering: Organizational Transformation." *Infoline* No. 259308.

Estep, T. (2004). "Organization Development for Trainers." *Infoline* No. 250411.

Gilley, J.W. (1992). "Strategic Planning for Human Resource Development." *Infoline* No. 259206. (Out of print.)

Koehle, D. (1997). "The Role of the Performance Change Manager." *Infoline* No. 259715.

Kotter, J.P. (1996). *Leading Change*. Boston: Harvard Business School Press.

Prochaska, J.O., J. Norcross, and C. DiClemente. (1994). *Changing for Good*. New York: William Morrow and Company.

Rose, E., and S. Buckley. (1999). *Self-Directed Work Teams*. Alexandria, VA: ASTD Press.

Scott, B. (2000). *Consulting on the Inside*. Alexandria, VA: ASTD Press.

Shaffer, R. (1988). "Principles of Organizational Development." *Infoline* No. 258812. (Out of print.)

Smith, W. (1989). "Managing Change: Implementation Skills." *Infoline* No. 258910. (Out of print.)

Willmore, J. (2004). *Performance Basics*. Alexandria, VA: ASTD Press.

7
Process Thinking and Design

 There are many process strategies that organizations may choose to incorporate. These vary by the nature of the business. These tools provide processes that can be used to consistently make decisions and resolve difficult situations. There is also a systematic standard for implementing projects using the project life cycle, which maximizes acceptance, minimizes risk, and allows for effective contingency planning. The goal for the training organization is to first get a seat at the planning table to be involved in the change process from conception. The training team should be able to provide the return-on-investment on the programs and effectively communicate the success measures that are applicable and align with the needs of the stakeholders.

Business process analysis is a structured method of documenting business rules and functions to uncover hidden inefficiencies that highlight strengths that could be streamlined or leveraged to increase productivity. Business process analysis attempts to standardize work flows in a manner that decreases redundancy of effort and increases information reuse. By conducting a business process analysis at an organization, the requirements for effectively and efficiently capturing, storing, retrieving, and managing knowledge can be implemented in an organization.

Business process analysis and design is often a prerequisite for new projects. So what is a business process? A process is how people, materials, methods, machines, and the environment combine to add value to a product or service. Everything that gets done is a part of the process—how the work gets done, roles and responsibilities, and resources and systems.

Process mapping is a workflow diagram that offers a clearer understanding of a process or series of parallel processes. Process mapping entails constructing a process flowchart to determine where processes begin and end. The process map can show only the required information (general process flow) or detail every finite action and decision point. The purpose of process mapping is to use diagramming to understand the process currently used and to identify appropriate benchmarks for measuring process results.

Process mapping must occur before process redesign, an initiative designed to change the flow of activities or decisions that are associated with generating a specific business output, can be implemented. Examples of business outputs include a design for a new product, purchase order, and service. Although business outputs may often be produced in one department, many of an organization's mission-critical processes span departmental boundaries.

Learning Objective:

☑ Define business process, and list and define the characteristics of business process analysis and design.

Key Knowledge: Process Thinking

Business process analysis, design, and redesign document workflow activities and decisions. Well-designed work flows tend to

- involve groups of people who are responsible for executing the tasks

- use a diagramming method (such as process maps or flowcharts) to pictorially display current and future flows of activities and decisions among departments

- use metrics to establish performance baselines and measure progress

- incorporate whole-systems thinking so that process performance is aligned with other organizational variables, such as overall strategy, competitive pressures, and activities in other parts of the organization.

Many initiatives seek to redesign processes, including total quality management and business reengineering. In addition, systems thinking projects often result in changes to organizational processes. Process analysis and redesign are appropriate initiatives when one or more of the following root causes is attributed to the performance problem:

- Department changes of information or materials are slow, cumbersome, and inefficient.

- Decisions take longer than they should and are of low quality.

- A string of process activities that span departmental boundaries is not managed well because of turn issues that arise in the execution of the process.

- Bottleneck areas cause delays.

- Benchmarking data from either inside or outside the organization suggests that outputs might be generated faster, cheaper, or with higher quality.

- The spirit and culture of continuous improvement exists in the organization, and people actively seek opportunities to redesign existing work flows.

The methodology used to identify, clarify, and improve business processes consists of a variety of problem-solving and quantitative tools and techniques. In many large organizations, considerable time and energy is initially spent defining the beginning and ending boundaries of preliminary business processes (that is, where the process begins and ends). This enables a business process to be seen as a logical, manageable piece in a complex organizational task.

For more information, see Module 8, *Managing Organizational Knowledge*, chapter 5, "Business Process Analysis."

8
Engagement Practices

Performance is never a solo act. The active support and participation of others is always required to achieve business or organizational goals. Those others may be reporting employees, peers, upper-level managers, or anyone with a stake in the project or decision. The ability to use standard problem-solving methodologies is critical as companies and organizations focus more and more on root-cause analysis. Engaging others to actively participate in the identification, solution, and assessment of problems and issues is a critical success factor.

Learning Objectives:

☑ List the steps of performing a needs analysis to define a need for change.

☑ Explain the Six Sigma practices for presenting and measuring the effect on business or performance before a change.

☑ Define best practices for communicating issues to the workforce.

☑ Examine the importance of owning the process.

Needs Analysis for Change

Before an organization can transform itself, it must recognize the need to do so. That sounds straightforward; however, failure to recognize the need for change is among the most common barriers to a company's adapting to the new requirements of a global marketplace. "We've always done it this way." "It has always worked before." "If it ain't broke, don't fix it." Those attitudes are roadblocks on the way to change. Management commitment of resources is critical to the success of any organizational transformation.

Managers must develop a clear vision of where they want to lead their organizations and a plan for accomplishing it. The first step is to break from old, self-limiting paradigms. Those preconceived ways of looking at the world are major barriers to performance. Lasting change requires adjustment of the organization's culture—changes to its shared expectations, values, and beliefs.

Identifying the gap between actual and desired performance is critical to ensure that the change initiative design is tailored to bridge the gaps. Such initiatives that are designed to bridge performance and learning gaps add value and, ultimately, move the business in a positive direction. These steps will help ensure that the needs assessment process will ultimately lead the organization to its desired goals:

- Conduct external and organizational scans.
- Collect data to identify business needs.
- Identify potential change initiatives.
- Collect data to identify performance, learning, and learner needs.
- Analyze the data.
- Deliver data analysis feedback.
- Begin designing the change initiative.

Six Sigma Practices for Change

Strategic Six Sigma principles and practices, as mentioned in chapter 4, can help companies formulate and integrate business strategies and missions and drive revenue growth, among other things.

Six Sigma is a high-performing, data-driven approach to analyzing and solving root causes of business problems. It ties the outputs of a business directly to marketplace requirements. At the strategic or transformative level, the goal of Six Sigma is to align an organization with its marketplace and deliver real improvements and dollars to the bottom line.

At the operational or transactional level, Six Sigma's goal is to move business product or service attributes within the zone of customer specifications and dramatically shrink process variation—the cause of defects that negatively affect customers. It provides specific tools and approaches (process analysis, statistical analysis, lean techniques, and root-cause methods) that can be used to reduce defects and dramatically improve processes to increase customer satisfaction and drive down costs.

For Six Sigma to succeed in organizations, individual leaders must develop competencies in statistical data analysis and process redesign, and be able to cascade those approaches to other levels of leaders inside the organization.

Training practitioners have a huge opportunity to be involved in coaching their companies' leaders on how to deploy Six Sigma successfully and in helping to transform the culture and operating systems of their organizations. The training that is needed to give leaders of Six Sigma appropriate skills is intensive, but the payoffs are enormous.

Communicating Issues to the Workforce

Clear, unambiguous communications are vital for success in any venture. Communication refers to the nature of interactions within and outside an organization, and to the way that members handle conflict, decision making, and day-to-day interactions. Communication also promotes intrinsic motivation by giving feedback to workers.

Multiple Forms of Media

The following are effective ways to communicate a change strategy.

- Meetings are one way to communicate change. Types of meetings include
  - all-employee meetings, scheduled on a regular basis or as needed
  - leadership meetings, scheduled on a regular basis or as needed
  - quick focus sessions (for example, lesson-learned session after project completion or team initiative)
  - department huddles (that is, impromptu, informal department gatherings for giving information, celebrating, or reinforcing morale).
- Telephone coaching is another way to relate the change. Potential coaches—which include HR staff, internal SMEs, and external consultant experts—can coach on performance, careers, or processes.
- Performance, career, and process coaches can use on-site coaching with groups or individuals. Potential coaches include human resources staff, internal subject matter experts, and external consultant experts.
- Additional communication vehicles are
  - newsletters
  - department bulletin boards
  - intranet bulletin boards
  - all-employee letters.

- Another method to communicate change is telephone hotlines, at which employees submit questions, share challenges and successes, and request information.

- Training activities include

  - classroom, on-the-job, or self-instructional (for example, workbook, video, CD-ROM, or Internet-based) training for technical or behavioral issues

  - knowledge or information partnerships

  - learning contracts

  - action plan for transferring learning

  - peer teaching.

- Tools and models help develop skills transfer knowledge and provide a means for applying learning.

- A nerve center is a group containing key personnel, technology, and resources for deploying and coordinating change leadership tactics across an organization.

- A survival kit provides application-oriented tips and resources for coping with an organizational change.

- *Recognition days or weeks* can include these activities and items:

  - leadership and co-worker acknowledgment of employee contributions

  - banners, certificates, and profiles in the organization's newsletter recognizing achievements

  - nonmonetary rewards, such as flextime, compressed workweeks, special assignments, resources or technology, and special partnerships.

Status—What Is Going On?

For employees to understand and recognize the need for change, they must first know where the organization is currently, and where it needs to go. Communicating the current state of the company—a state-of-the-organization address from upper management, for example—is an effective means for team members to understand the value of the impending change.

How Are Measures Working?

When an organization implements a change initiative, it must also set in place specific measures to evaluate the effectiveness of the initiative. There must be a set of measurement tools that assess performance, process, skills, and knowledge effects. General measures apply to all functions of the change process and may include

- client and employee satisfaction

- financial effects

- performance and process improvements

- skills and knowledge improvement.

Owning the Process

The details of the change management plan should spell out how employees will be personally involved in the change, as involvement is one way to foster commitment to the change. Although the change plan lays out where the organization needs to go and what the organization will do as a whole to get there, employees will need to decide how the work processes are redesigned to meet changing needs. This involvement allows employees to increase learning and problem-solving skills. The effort to redesign work also provides employees with opportunities to work through the feelings and emotions that are part of adapting to change.

✓ **Chapter 8 Knowledge Check**

1. **Six Sigma's goal is to move business product or service attributes within the zone of customer specifications and dramatically shrink process variation—the cause of defects that negatively affect customers. Six Sigma may be an effective technique to use in change initiatives because**

    __ **A.** It provides specific tools and approaches that can be used to reduce defects and improve processes

    __ **B.** It facilitates change by getting everyone involved

    __ **C.** It focuses on identifying the best of what is

    __ **D.** It outlines how to conduct a communication audit and how to create a communication plan

2. **Six Sigma is a high-performance, data-driven approach to analyzing and solving root causes and problems.**

    __ **A.** True

    __ **B.** False

3. **The training department has been asked to join a group attempting to implement Six Sigma processes into their organization. The implementation team is in the beginning stages of review but is looking for input from the training department. At this stage of implementation, where can the training department have the greatest effect in supporting the Six Sigma initiative?**

    __ **A.** Coaching leaders on how to implement Six Sigma

    __ **B.** Managing the transition to Six Sigma processes

    __ **C.** Creating Six Sigma processes within training and development

    __ **D.** Developing leadership models that Six Sigma can flourish within

4. **One effective strategy used to introduce change in an organization is to select a single media and style to communicate the change.**

    __ **A.** True

    __ **B.** False

5. **A WLP professional is preparing a communication plan to distribute a list of critical issues regarding the change strategy to employees. Of the following examples, which is *not* a recognized media venue for communication?**

    __ **A.** Teleconferences to provide an ongoing roadmap to managers

    __ **B.** A change survivor's guide to help people through change

    __ **C.** A telephone hotline for the latest breaking news and information

    __ **D.** An experiential learning activity that involves outdoor physical activities

6. **A change management plan should spell out how employees will be personally involved and compensated to help foster commitment.**

   __ **A.** True

   __ **B.** False

---

7. **A WLP professional is discussing the importance of involving employees to aid the change process. Which of the following is the best reason for involving employees in change?**

   __ **A.** It helps people to become committed to the change.

   __ **B.** Everyone needs to feel wanted and needed.

   __ **C.** Stressful times can often spark feelings of isolation.

   __ **D.** It provides a vehicle of expression for employees.

References

Cowan, S.L. (1999). "Change Management." *Infoline* No. 259904.

Koehle, D. (1997). "The Role of the Performance Change Manager." *Infoline* No. 259715.

Rose, E., and S. Buckley. (1999). *Self-Directed Work Teams*. Alexandria, VA: ASTD Press.

Smith, D., and J. Blakesell. (September 2002). "The New Strategic Six Sigma," *T+D*, pp. 45–52.

Willmore, J. (2004.) *Performance Basics*. Alexandria, VA: ASTD Press.

9
Communication Theory

Success in organizational change is directly proportionate to the level of effective communication. It is helpful to know the participants and apply the appropriate communication style(s), which is an art. Understanding the art of effective communication is the foundation for change, and confidence in verbal communication helps to sell the change plan. Clear and concise written communication is also critical and greatly contributes to credibility and alignment.

Learning Objectives:

☑ Explain how communication relates to facilitating change.

☑ Define common communication styles.

☑ List and describe a variety of communication channels.

Communication and Facilitating Change

Oral expression—together with its nonverbal components—is a very important communication skill. Every time communication takes place, people convey something of who they are and what they think. Vocabulary, grammar, phrasing, tone, eye contact, body movement, and gestures all make impressions on those with whom one is communicating. If this impression is negative or poor, no matter how great the ideas are, the message will suffer. How many good ideas are ignored or misunderstood because their presenter simply could not communicate these ideas well?

This chapter provides pointers and techniques on how to communicate effectively, use nonverbal cues, and avoid common communication pitfalls. To facilitate change in an organization, an organizational development practitioner must be aware of the intricacies of communication so the message is not misinterpreted, or, worse, ignored altogether!

Sending and Receiving Messages

Information theory grew out of scientists' interest in electronic communication systems. As mathematicians and engineers developed information theory (also called communication theory), it came to be applied to nonelectronic systems, including those for human information processing. Listening is now described as one activity in a relational process; speaking is the other. Together they make a dyadic (two-part) system. These are some of the concepts and terms practitioners and researchers in these areas use:

- *environment:* conditions or circumstances within which a system operates

- *information:* something that reduces uncertainty

- *message:* something that is communicated

- *sender:* the person communicating a message

- *noise or filter:* something that hinders the flow of information between a source and a receiver

- *receiver:* a person or device that gets a message in human communications and processes it through the filter of the mind

- *feedback:* a communication that gives a person information about the effect of his or her behavior on others.

There are many things that get in the way of dialog reception and message interpretation. Miscommunications, censored feedback, and poor listening can diminish a conversation or communication. A person may not hear what someone is saying even if he or she hears the words being spoken. Communication between two people goes through each person's filters. Figure 9-1 displays the **sender-receiver model** and shows how messages change as they pass through the filters (mindset, biases, and opinions) of the sender and receiver.

Even with the best of intentions, messages can become distorted and confused.

Figure 9-1. Sender-Receiver Model

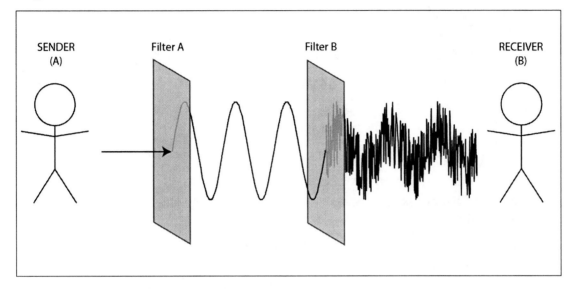

Barriers and Obstacles

"Listening, really listening, is tough and grinding work, often humbling, sometimes distasteful," says author Robert H. Waterman Jr. in *The Renewal Factor: How to Get and Keep the Competitive Edge* (1987). When good listeners are on the receiving end of a message, they may come up against many barriers to understanding; awareness of them is the first step to avoiding mistakes.

The rate at which a typical speaker talks (about 120 to 180 words per minute) and the rate a listener can understand (from about 280 to 560 words per minute) is exploited by TV and radio commercials using electronically altered speech to tell and sell listeners more. Some speakers, such as auctioneers, talk at a rate of speed that is much faster than the average listener can comprehend. With practice, even this fast-talking style can be understood. Most people can think three times faster than the person who is sending the message. If the typical speaker simply talks faster, however, the words sound rushed or anxious. Other problems may originate with the speaker because the speaker

- may be reluctant to convey the message
- has not thought the message through
- is misinformed or lying
- has speech difficulties
- has an accent different from that of the listener
- lacks the vocabulary to explain the matter at hand or, conversely, uses highly specialized jargon that the listener cannot decode
- uses nonverbal communication that does not support his or her words
- fails to state early on why the message may be of importance to the listener.

However, a listener may

- be preoccupied and may not shift from this internal dialog to the external conversation

- be distracted by positive or negative emotional trigger words

- feel on the defensive and concentrate on a rebuttal or counterattack before getting the whole message

- be distracted by reactions to the speaker's clothes, hair style, and so forth

- feel superior to and disrespectful of the speaker

- be impatient and interrupt because that person has other pressing business, believes this message is a waste of time, and suspects the message will be unpleasant

- lack the vocabulary or understanding of nonverbal communication needed to interpret the message

- have impaired hearing—although a profoundly deaf person can be a good listener in the sense of mental and emotional receptiveness to messages from others.

Other potential barriers to understanding include a physically uncomfortable or disruptive setting, or too much distance between the speaker and the listeners.

To better understand what another person is saying, the listener may ask him or her to come back at a more convenient or specific time. Waiting until they can both move to a less distracting place, the door can be closed, or phone calls held will create a setting that enhances rather than inhibits understanding. Also, rephrasing, defining, or elaborating on part of the message clarifies that the listener has interpreted the speaker's meaning correctly.

The listener may also work to keep an open mind about the content and value of the whole message. Listeners should avoid being sidetracked by reactions to appearance, accent, and emotional trigger words. Attention to the speaker's nonverbal communication is equally important. Lastly, the listener should find a position conducive to listening—choosing to stand or sit near the speaker, away from scenic views, clocks, and other distractions.

Deciding What to Communicate

The first step in effective communication is deciding what needs to be communicated to someone. It can be helpful to make a list of items to be addressed then formulate fuller ideas based on those items. There should be logical segues between conversation points so that the communication flows smoothly and in a way that makes sense. If information about a change is communicated in an unmanaged fashion, it becomes diffused, less specific, and interpreted in arbitrary ways. Additionally, it is important to avoid rhetoric. Problems occur when people say one thing, but their behavior or actions suggest the opposite.

When communicating change initiatives to others, there are three points that will help ensure all involved understand:

- *Tell them in advance:* People do not like surprises, so springing some unexpected change on employees can create a sense of panic. Be sure that people know in advance that a change is coming so they have time to prepare for it.

- *Give enough information:* Vague language should always be avoided in communication. Wait until all points are clear before communicating them to someone else.

- *Ensure messages correspond with actions:* This is also called walking the talk. It's imperative in business communication to make sure that verbal or written communiqués are reflected in subsequent actions.

Deciding How to Communicate It

Communication is just as much about human relationships as it is about sharing information. This creates a more open forum for open dialog. Options for communication include written communiqués, one-on-one meetings, or group meetings. Each communication can be evaluated to decide which format is most suited to the communication. If the information is in regard to a specific individual, for instance, the discussion should not take place in front of others. One-on-one communication is more effective, especially if there are any negatives involved. If such a communication takes place in front of others, that person will not perceive it as constructive criticism, rather that person will be embarrassed or even angry for having that information exposed in front of others.

Anticipating the Receiver's Perspective

When communicating a change initiative, consider how the change will affect the people involved. Some may be excited, some may be fearful, others may simply be confused. When communicating, it is important to pay attention to the listener's body language. Does he or she seem apprehensive? Excited? Thoughtful? Knowing how people respond to communication helps to ensure that the proper message gets across. Additionally, honing listening skills can help in understanding the receiver's perspective. Some pointers for competent listening include

- making eye contact

- assuming the listening position—sitting up straight, leaning forward, taking notes

- listening with enjoyment

- giving undivided attention

- asking questions.

Communication Styles

There are a variety of methods for effective communication. The following sections discuss some of the more common forms of communication, with pointers on how to use each effectively.

Verbal

A good voice is the primary means by which information can be imparted from one person to another or to a group. It has three important characteristics: quality, intelligibility, and variability.

Quality

Voice quality is the overall impression that a voice makes on its listeners. Some voices have a full, rich quality, while others may be shrill and nasal or breathy and muffled. Often, listeners can read emotions from the sound of someone's voice alone. Although some people focus too heavily on the basic quality of their voices, it makes more sense to pay attention to something that can be changed—the voice's amazing ability to display emotion and attitude.

Intelligibility

Voice intelligibility, or understandability, depends on several factors:

- *Articulation:* Articulation or enunciation is the precision and clarity with which the sounds of speech are uttered. Articulation is chiefly the job of the jaw, tongue, and lips; most articulation problems come from simple laziness on the parts of these organs.

- *Pronunciation:* This refers to the traditional or customary utterance of words. Standards differ from place to place and from time to time. Dictionaries may be useful, but they become outdated and should not be followed compulsively. Common pronunciation faults are misplacement of the accent, omitting sounds, adding sounds, and verbalizing silent letters. Pronunciation acceptable in informal conversation may be considered substandard in a public presentation.

- *Vocalized pauses:* This is the name given to the syllables "uh," "um," and "ah" often found at the beginning of a spoken sentence. Although a few vocalized pauses are natural and do not distract, too many can impede the communication process. Knowing the subject and planning what to say is one way to minimize this problem.

- *Overuse of stock expressions:* This includes things such as "OK," "like," and "you know"; avoid these as much as possible. These expressions serve no positive communication function and convey callowness and a lack of originality.

- *Substandard grammar:* Using incorrect grammar is almost always unacceptable when speaking. Using it reduces credibility with some listeners, clouds meaning, and distracts listeners from what is really being said. Research has shown that even those who have used substandard grammar their entire lives can, with diligent practice, improve their skills significantly in a relatively short time.

Variability

Voice variability expresses differences in meaning. Like salt and pepper on food, variety spices up speech. A speaker's voice with good quality still may not appeal to listeners if that voice is used in a boring or monotonous way. Listeners rapidly tire of a voice that doesn't vary its delivery style. Vocal fundamentals, such as rate, volume, force, pitch, and emphasis, will vary a voice and, thus, improve communication.

- *Rate:* This measures words spoken per minute. In a typical presentation, most people speak an average of 140 words per minute. Even within this average, however, speakers vary their rates of speech to emphasize specific ideas and feelings. For example, a slower rate may be appropriate for presenting main points or serious topics, while a more rapid pace may lend itself to support more lighthearted material. The experienced speaker also knows that an occasional pause in the flow of speech punctuates thoughts and emphasizes ideas. A dramatic pause at the proper time may express feelings and ideas even more effectively than words.

- *Volume:* How easily a voice is heard is crucial to any presentation. All participants must be able to hear to benefit from the speech. Asking someone in the back row if he or she can hear is the best way to assess this, and the listeners will appreciate the conscientiousness.

- *Force:* This is also referred to as variability of volume and is needed at times to emphasize or dramatize ideas and improve communication. Of course, using force doesn't always mean getting louder. A sudden reduction in force may be as effective as a rapid increase. In either situation, a drowsy listener will snap to attention quickly if force is used effectively.

- *Pitch:* This is the highness or lowness of a voice. All other things being equal, a higher-pitched voice carries better than a lower-pitched one. Listeners, however, tend to tire more quickly when listening to a higher-pitched voice.

- *Emphasis:* Stressing certain phrases or sections obviously stems from all forms of vocal variety, and any change in rate, force, or pitch influences the emphasis. The greater or more sudden the change, the greater the emphasis will be. A speaker uses emphasis wisely. Two strategies to avoid are overemphasis and continual emphasis. Emphasizing a point beyond its real value may cost credibility with listeners. And continual emphasis is as deadly boring and self-defeating as no emphasis at all.

Five Levels of Listening

Communication is a complex process that involves different levels of listening. Table 9-1 starts with the most basic, nonverbal behaviors and evolves to high-level behaviors that signify a more intense, meaningful level of listening and connecting.

Communicating Change

According to a study by the Harvard Business School, strategic communication is critical when implementing long-term changes. Such communication is part education and part marketing. Change leaders should consider such an implementation in the same light as a new product, focusing on how to convince customers that they need it and building trust and loyalty in the new product. Strategic communication necessitates evaluating what it is employees need to do and persuading them why it is in their best interest to change behaviors. Change agents must merchandise the concept of change in a way that makes the desired changes relevant and appealing to those who must carry it out.

Additional considerations for such communications include providing periodic updates on how the change initiative is progressing and selecting proper communication channels for communication.

Speaking Versus Writing

Although speaking and writing are both forms of communication, the two differ in several important ways:

Table 9-1. The Five Levels of Listening

Level of Listening	Characteristics
Passive listening	Demonstrating nonverbal behaviors, such as affirmative head nodding, eye contact, note taking, smiling, or presenting a thinking pose at appropriate moments
Listening for knowledge	Listening first for facts and logic and then mentally listing things in a sequence or pattern to form conclusions
Active listening	Demonstrating appropriate nonverbal behaviors that are responsive to questions posed or asking questions to increase understanding
Listening for clarification	Paraphrasing and replaying in different words to help the listeners increase their understanding of the previous comments and dialog
Empathetic listening	Identifying feelings by confirming with the listener if an intuition about his or her feelings is correct

- *Level of diction:* In speaking, simple vocabulary and short sentences are more quickly understood by listeners. Listeners do not have the time or mechanisms to review what was said without potentially missing what follows.

- *Amount of repetition:* Aside from voice variability, speech has no italics or boldface print. The best way to do this is to repeat key phrases and words to emphasize or summarize these important points.

- *Kinds of transitions:* Transitions from one idea to another must be explicit in verbal communication. Speeches do not have headers and paragraphs to let their listeners know where the narrative breaks are. Voice variability is one way to show these breaks—for example, "The second most serious issue is. . . ."

- *Kinds of visuals:* Public speaking readily lends itself to the use of graphics, maybe even more than the printed page. Complex images can be explained at length. Pieces of the material can be easily highlighted or emphasized. And, graphics can be modified or can incorporate motion during the explanation.

Nonverbal

Communication experts believe that more than half of all communication may be nonverbal. As mentioned previously, vocal clues communicate much of this nonverbal meaning. However, a great deal of meaning is also transmitted by physical appearance, including such behaviors as eye contact, body movement, and gestures.

Movement and Language

Static speakers are boring. Moving around the stage or platform effectively catches the eye of the listener. Movement helps hold the listener's attention, and it can show a marked departure or change in the delivery that punctuates and paragraphs the message.

How much movement is desirable? Although some effective speakers never move, this situation is rare. The only reasons not to move are speaking in a highly formal situation or in which there is a fixed microphone.

Of course, some speakers move too much, either racing pointlessly to and fro, or pacing back and forth in front of their listeners. Still others have awkward movements that do not aid communication. For example, some leave their notes on the lectern, then move in and out from behind it like a child playing hide-and-seek; others plant their feet firmly in one place, then rock from one side to the other in regular cadence. These bad habits are easy to learn and just as easy to break.

Gestures

Gesturing is the purposeful use of hands, arms, shoulders, and head to reinforce what someone is saying. Used appropriately, gestures can clarify or emphasize pieces of the presentation.

Effective gestures are complete and vigorous. Many speakers begin to gesture but then stop suddenly, perhaps fearing they look ridiculous. Ironically, the listeners will notice the aborted gesture. Aborted gestures convey nervousness and a lack of confidence. Naturally effective gestures come simultaneously or slightly before their verbal cues. Poor timing results from preplanned gestures, the effect of which can best be described as unfortunately comic.

Finally, good gestures are versatile. A stereotyped gesture will not fit all subjects and situations. In fact, the larger the crowd, the more pronounced the gestures need to be. As with body movement, gestures should spring from within and at least appear both natural and spontaneous.

Eye Contact

Eye contact is a crucial factor in good nonverbal communication because

- A majority of listeners want a speaker to look at them during at least part of the presentation.

- Effective eye contact enhances credibility. Speakers who demonstrate better eye contact with their listeners usually strike the listeners as more competent and more in control. Old advice, such as looking over the tops of listeners' heads or systematically glancing at parts of the crowd, is not effective eye contact. Furthermore, looking directly at only one part of the crowd—especially only those listeners who give reinforcing feedback—can cause the presenter to ignore the other parts of the crowd.

The most effective eye contact can be described as direct and impartial.

Written Communication

Clear, concise written communication is one of the most critical skills in business today. Change managers must be able to fully communicate the details of a change initiative to employees in a way that states objectives, identifies intended outcomes, and clearly communicates all details of the initiative.

When crafting written communication, change managers should first establish a clear objective: What should the readers take away from the communication? Once the objective is defined, change managers should stick to it so readers know what their responsibilities are as a result of the communication. They should always streamline written communication so it clearly states objectives and expectations.

Change managers should target the listeners appropriately. They should consider the people who will be reading the communication to identify how to motivate the readers to do what it is that is required of them. Finally, change managers should assess the situation, environment, needs, and communication style of others to match their preferences in the delivery of information.

Influencing in Writing

Leaders are only as successful as their ability to communicate ideas, knowledge, and information. Communication skills are essential in developing the skills of others as well as in creating relationships based upon collaboration. Teams, work groups, and separate organizations rely on each other to deliver results. Getting shared results depends on strong communication skills and the leader's ability to influence across functions.

To influence others, it is crucial to explain decisions and reasoning and invite questions. Successful communication builds relationships based on asking questions and sharing ideas. Influencing across functions involves the ability to call upon resources across an organization. This ability is important because today's organizations operate as a connected whole. Projects require sharing of resources to be successful. Cross-organizational influence depends on creating relationships throughout the organization as well as developing an environment that reinforces collaboration.

Selecting Media in Which to Communicate

Messages can be sent through a variety of communication media or channels, including face-to-face, written, electronic, and telephone. Any of these methods of communication can range from formal to informal. The context and the listeners determine the level of formality to be adopted.

Written communication also has degrees of formality. Email tends to be the current preferred communication channel. However, the convenience of email as a written form of communication makes it dangerous. Many people are careless with email communications, overlooking the intentions of their messages and sending thoughts that can be misinterpreted. Unless carefully crafted, email lacks a clear feeling, so the reader must apply his or her own tone of voice interpretation to the words. Problems occur when the receiver's interpretation of tone does not match the sender's intended tone.

Communicating to Diverse Workforces

Communicating to a diverse group can be enhanced by these four steps:

1. *Assessment:* When communicating with someone of another culture, both parties have to assess the importance of the respective cultures in the communication. This includes what assumptions are common in the culture, as well as gestures and language used.

2. *Acknowledgment:* The communicators must recognize not only the cultural biases of the other party, but also their own.

3. *Attitude:* Flexibility is required when dealing with individuals from other cultures. Some adjustment in the individual's assumptions or approach may be necessary to develop an atmosphere conducive to conflict-free communications.

4. *Action:* The communicator can take several steps to ensure better communications. These include the following behaviors:

- *Establishing credibility:* Rather than approaching a communication with a list of cultural dos and don'ts, be curious. Ask questions about differences in language, environment, technology, thought processing, and gestures.

- *Gaining trust:* Recognize and act on the principles that convey trust in the specific cultures involved.

- *Maintaining accurate communications:* Recognize that the "what you heard isn't what I meant" adage is apt when dealing across languages. Slang and jargon often do not translate into foreign tongues.

- *Anticipating reactions:* Acquire as much knowledge as possible about the culture from which the other comes. This acquisition is ongoing—learn as much as possible both before and during the meeting.

- *Giving feedback:* Providing and getting feedback about communication techniques implies an interest in and concern for the other party, as well as allowing the communicator to collect more data about the other culture, the other party's way of thinking, and whether the conversation is low or high context.

- *Remaining flexible:* The ability to adapt to or understand the other's culture is mandatory. Flexibility and the facility for remaining nonjudgmental are the fundamentals of open communication.

Communication Channels

The change manager can help facilitate change acceptance by having a thorough knowledge of how communication moves through the organization. One way to achieve that understanding is by conducting a communication audit. The communication audit will reveal where communication breakdowns occur. It will also note how the formal communication media is received. Such an audit generally consists of information interviews, focus groups, surveys, policy and procedures review, and operations observation. Particular attention needs to be paid to the informal communication networks, which can facilitate or sabotage change efforts.

The information from interviews and focus groups is helpful in understanding the communications environment and will help define what types of questions should be asked in the survey. Questions for information interviews and focus groups cover such topics as

- what messages are being received

- message credibility

- how the leadership is perceived

- how information moves through the organization, the quality and quantity of information provided

- the preferred sources of information compared to the actual sources

- what forms of media are preferred for different types of messages.

Based on information gathered during the interviews and focus groups, the survey is designed and pretested. In addition to gathering data on the communications environment, it is important to ask demographic questions, such as length of service and work location, to determine if any particular employee group or area falls outside the norm.

Where demographics indicate a problem, additional communication resources can be allocated. Where demographics indicate an above average communications environment, steps can be taken to learn what is at work and whether any useful ideas can be borrowed for use in other areas of the organization.

Defining informal communication networks can be achieved by performing a network analysis. Generally, there are six types of informal networks:

1. *Advice networks:* These are networks used to solve problems.

2. *Trust networks:* These networks are those where sensitive information is shared.

3. *Communication networks:* These networks are used for discussing work-related matters.

4. *Information networks:* These networks are composed of those who share information with each other and are where to focus when there is a need to transform technical systems.

5. *Influence networks:* These focus on the political side of the organization and can be used to change the distribution of power within the organization.

6. *Affect networks:* These networks are those of friendships within the organization and are closely connected to the corporate culture. If there is a high degree of political uncertainty in an organization, it is nearly impossible to address technical or cultural issues. This makes it all the more imperative that the political players are brought into the change process early and are supportive of it.

During the network analysis, questions to ask include these:

- Whom do you trust?

- Whom do you talk to for work advice?

- Whom do you go to when you need a problem solved?

- Whom do you go to when you want information about what's going on in the company?

Because trust is such an important element to both change management and open communication, valuable information might be gained by asking, "Whom don't you trust?" In an audit, it is a good idea to determine what the trust level is within the organization. Employees need to feel a high degree of trust to move through the change acceptance stages. Attempts to introduce change into organizations with serious trust problems are likely to fail. If a communication audit finds trust problems, increasing the level of trust will need to be one of the first steps in the change management plan.

Change managers can use informal networks to advance the change agenda by helping bring together groups to serve as teams or task forces in a way that takes advantage of new and old alliances.

Based on the results of a completed audit, a formal change communication plan can be developed. The plan should define objectives, identify the listeners, define the key messages, determine the media and timing for delivering the messages, and define what feedback mechanisms will be used to evaluate how the message is being received.

Powerbases

A powerbase is where organizational power emanates and how it is used. Understanding where power lies and how it is used is an important aspect of implementing a change initiative. There are a number of types of power at work in organizations:

- *Reward power:* This is the ability to deliver positive consequences or remove negative consequences.

- *Coercive power:* This is the ability to give out negative consequences or remove positive consequences.

- *Legitimate power:* This is due to position in the group or organization or career (police, for example).

- *Reverent power:* This type of power is personality based—people like the person and identify with the individual.

- *Expert power:* This type of power comes from being seen as having special knowledge or skills and being trustworthy. (If expertise fosters feelings of inadequacy, it will have negative effects.)

- *Informational power:* This type of power is based on the belief that the person has resources of information that may be useful to accomplish a goal.

To understand how to leverage power in an organization, it is important to understand which powerbase is the most prevalent and which powerbases are in use in the organization.

✓ Chapter 9 Knowledge Check

1. **In the sender-receiver model, which term best describes any mindsets, opinions, or biases that may affect how the communication is received?**

   ___ **A.** Feedback

   ___ **B.** Distraction

   ⟍ **C.** Filter

   ___ **D.** Innapropriate nonverbal communication

2. **Which of the following is *not* a barrier to communication?**

   ___ **A.** Rate of speech

   ___ **B.** Speech difficulties

   ___ **C.** Physically uncomfortable environment

   ⟍ **D.** Written communication

3. **When communicating change initiatives to others, which of the following is *not* one of the key points that will help ensure all involved understand?**

   ⟍ **A.** Provide information at the outset of change initiative

   ⟍ **B.** Provide advance notice

   ___ **C.** Give thorough and complete information

   ___ **D.** Ensure messages correspond with actions

4. **A WLP professional is providing a peer assessment on a co-worker in the same role. During the feedback process, the WLP professional receiving the feedback politely asks if it is OK if she multitasks and sends a few email messages. What of the following are potential problems with this strategy? (Choose the option that poses the greatest risk to the communication between the two WLP professionals.)**

   ___ **A.** Lack of vocabulary understanding between the two WLP professionals

   ___ **B.** Failure to point out the importance of the message to the listener

   ___ **C.** Feelings of defensiveness and rebuttal between the two WLP professionals

   ⟍ **D.** A disruptive setting that is a challenge to both WLP professionals communicating

5. **Voice intelligibility, or understandability, depends on several factors. Which of the factors is best described as expressions that serve no positive communications function, such as "OK," "like," and "you know"?**

   __ **A.** Vocalized pauses

   __ **B.** Overuse of stock expressions

   __ **C.** Substandard grammar

   __ **D.** Force

6. **Using gestures always enhances communication and relaying of messages.**

   __ **A.** True

   __ **B.** False

7. **A WLP professional is facilitating a meeting with key stakeholders. The meeting begins with the facilitator making the following presentation: "Good morning, uh, thanks for coming today. Uh, I am, uh, especially thankful for, uh, your participation in, uh, our discussion today about training methodologies." The intelligibility issue exhibited in this situation can best be characterized as what type of factor?**

   __ **A.** Articulation

   __ **B.** Vocalized pauses

   __ **C.** Pronunciation

   __ **D.** Overuse of stock expressions

8. **One way a change manager can help facilitate change acceptance is by having thorough knowledge of how communication moves through an organization. One technique used to identify this flow and where communication breakdowns occur is called a communication audit.**

   __ **A.** True

   __ **B.** False

9. **Informal networks can sabotage change efforts.**

   __ **A.** True

   __ **B.** False

10. **All of the following are examples of how a change manager can use an informal network *except* to**

___ **A.** Change the distribution of power in the organization

___ **B.** Help bring together groups to work as teams or taskforces

___ **C.** Discuss personal issues of specific individuals

___ **D.** Use informal networks in advance of meetings to change the agenda

11. **What is "noise" in the communication model described in this chapter?**

___ **A.** A barrier to communication

___ **B.** The communicated words

___ **C.** The soundwaves of the message

___ **D.** Any sounds outside of the actual message

References

Hambrick, D., D. Nadler, and M. Tushman. (1998). *Navigating Change*. Boston: Harvard Business School Press.

Jennings, J., and L. Malcak. (2004). *Communication Basics*. Alexandria, VA: ASTD Press.

Johnson, D., et al. (2005). *Joining Together: Group Theory and Group Skills* (5th edition). Boston: Allyn and Bacon.

Kirrane, D. (1988). "Listening to Learn: Learning to Listen." *Infoline* No. 258806. (Out of print.)

Koehle, D. (1997). "The Role of the Performance Change Manager." *Infoline* No. 259715.

Myers, S. (1990). "Basics of Intercultural Communication." *Infoline* No. 259009. (Out of print.)

Plattner, F.B. (1994). "Improve Your Communication Skills." *Infoline* No. 259409.

Russell, L. (2005). "Leadership Development." *Infoline* No. 250508.

Sindell, M. (2001). "Leadership Development." *Infoline* No. 250101. (Out of print.)

Waterman, R.H., Jr. (1987). *The Renewal Factor: How to Get and Keep the Competitive Edge*. New York: Bantam.

10
Diversity and Inclusion

 In an increasingly global work environment, everyone must develop and maintain an awareness of diversity. Diversity is a broad term illustrating distinct races, ethnicities, sexual orientations, faiths, age, and myriad other distinguishing factors that make each person unique. Acknowledging, accepting, and embracing diversity via inclusion ensures the effectiveness of decisions by providing broad opportunities to present and discuss diverging views.

A variety of approaches are used to maximize workplace diversity. Organizations use diversity initiatives to recognize the growing diversity of the workforce. It is important that there is awareness of the various aspects of diversity, and appropriate methods are put in place to meet strategic initiatives for a diverse population. Diversity initiatives should not only focus on race or ethnicity and gender, but also include age such as the different generations. For example, in today's workforce the baby boomer generation is getting ready to retire. Generations X and Y are poised to step into key managerial and leadership positions, which has significant implications for cultural change and even more awareness and acceptance of workers from various backgrounds, generations, and differing points of view. Instruments are available to assess workforce diversity. It is important that programs are developed that provide an awareness of diverse groups and population. Programs should also target global diversity and take this in consideration in career planning and talent management programs.

Organizations invest in diversity programs for a variety of reasons, with the changing demographics of the workforce being the most compelling. The Hudson Institute issued a striking forecast describing these changes, commonly known as the Workforce 2000 report. The institute's research suggests that women, immigrants, and minorities currently make up—and will continue to make up—a growing portion of new entries into the U.S. workforce. This literally changes the face and needs of the workforce and the consumer market.

Organizations that are betting on their workforces to help them with productivity, quality, flexibility, and innovation must understand what motivates all employees. What used to work does not work anymore. In addition, more businesses are competing in a global market. This economic focus requires skills in cross-cultural communication and necessitates valuing different cultural models.

Learning Objective:

☑ Discuss how diversity and inclusion programs and initiatives support organizational change.

Key Knowledge: Diversity and Inclusion

Many organizations lack a formal workforce training policy on the subject of diversity, even though its workforce reflects a racially and culturally diversified population. These organizations face potential racial discrimination lawsuits.

Organizational culture is socially constructed; it is created and changed through conversations. Culture involves the way people look at the world, a shared value system. It includes language but many other things as well, such as the value a society puts on individualism or group action, tolerance for uncertainty, willingness to take risks, and the comfort level in interacting with a teacher and peers. These and other factors have a direct effect on *learning styles* and how people interact on the job.

In countries like the United States, Canada, and Australia, learners are used to getting to the point quickly, while many Europeans may expect a more structured approach. Asians may prefer to master theory before digging into facts.

For managerial and leadership programs, training materials, ideally, might be entirely different for each country or culture and would take into account all issues of language, worldviews, learning styles, and content. However, this is rarely feasible. Instead, training materials and other software applications need to be designed from the start with multilingual and multicultural groups in mind and kept reasonably neutral.

These culture concepts and differences need to be considered when designing and delivering any training programs or change management initiatives—but especially in managerial and leadership development programs. Most organizations want to attract and retain a diverse workforce. Customers want to see themselves reflected within an organization. Attaining those objectives would not be possible without the implicit and informed support of leadership. To lend that support, workplace learning and performance (WLP) professionals need to provide education designed to help leaders and employees understand

- their responsibilities regarding diversity and inclusion management

- how developing and maintaining a diverse and inclusive environment supports the organization's mission and maintains and increases market share

- how increasing cultural competency makes a more effective leader and workforce

- how succession planning must include those who do not necessarily look or think like the current leadership.

A culture can enable or hinder success. WLP professionals can play a role in facilitating change by aligning development programs to reinforce the desired culture through conversations to change the culture for the better.

For more information, see Module 9, *Career Planning and Talent Management*, chapter 12, "Maximizing Workplace Diversity."

11
Motivation Theory

Change may be a business decision, but during transition there are significant emotional and political effects to consider on people, the human capital asset. Understanding what motivates employees varies but understanding motivating factors is perhaps the most critical element to consider while implementing organizational change. The effect could be resistance, turnover, and failure to institutionalize the change. Failure to maximize retention during a time of major change can also affect the quality of the change initiative outcome (result). Understanding how others are motivated can aid the manager to harness the potentially threatening resistance by some and transforming it into a favorable ally that stands as part of the solution. Empowering employees to make choices can help ensure the change is institutionalized. Management can contribute directly to motivation during this transition by rewarding those who have embraced change and provide additional support for those who have not.

Learning Objectives:

☑ Explain the best practices for motivating employees.

☑ Describe some considerations for motivating learners.

Motivation Best Practices

Motivating employees to achieve their potential is one of the most difficult challenges facing any manager or supervisor. Training managers and supervisors in employee **motivation theory** involves giving them the background they need to understand what motivation is and how to tap this drive among their employees.

Motivation is classically defined as the desire to work: the amount of effort put forth on a job. Everyone has a mindset that determines how and why they behave in a certain manner. These activities are based on motivational factors, such as personal goals, organizational and personal reward systems, and job enrichment.

In today's business climate, rewards and recognition have become more important than ever. Many managers, however, think that the only thing that motivates employees is money. Motivational experts agree that money is *not* the best way to motivate employees, yet according to management specialist and author Bob Nelson (1994), "It is a rare manager who systematically makes the effort simply to thank employees for a job well done, let alone to do something more innovative to recognize accomplishments."

Employee Motivators

When examining the workplace environment, there are two influences that have a great effect on the motivation of employees: management and performance.

Management

Instead of coming from some nebulous ad hoc committee or corporate institution, the most valuable recognition comes directly from a person's manager.

Rewarding Employees

Research into why talented people stay in organizations is the basis for the following ways for managers to show employees that they are appreciated. Workplace learning and performance (WLP) professionals should consider some of these activities to reward their employees:

Private Time With Managers

Have lunch with an employee and ask questions such as

- What can I do to keep you on my team?

- What might make your work life easier?

- What can I do to be more supportive or help you?

Frank Talk About the Future

Hold a career conversation in a quiet, private place—off-site, if possible. Ask these questions to start:

- What do you enjoy most about your job? The least?

- Which one of your talents have I not used yet?

- What jobs do you see yourself doing in the future?

Representing the Company

Give employees the chance to attend an outside conference or seminar designed for their affinity group.

Professional Growth

Let employees choose from a list of potential projects, assignments, or tasks that could enrich their work.

Recognizing Family

Give employees a prepaid phone card during the holiday season or a free pass for X number of days or hours off to attend children's school programs or sport activities.

Professional Interests

Give a subscription to an employee's favorite business magazine and satisfy employees' need for information.

Submit to Pruning

Ask an employee to engage in some straight talk about how to work together better. Listen carefully and do not become defensive. Then take a step toward changing at least one behavior.

A Unique Perk for Fun

Give an employee a coupon that entitles him or her to spend up to X dollars to take a break or have some fun at work. It could involve the entire team.

A Priceless Introduction

Ask the employee for the name of someone in the organization whom he or she would like to meet, chat with, and learn more about. Provide an introduction and encourage the employee to decide how to spend the time.

A Personal Trainer Session

Consider a gift certificate for an employee to have a lunch with a mentor of his or her choice.

A New Door

Brainstorm an opportunity hit list with an employee about growing, learning, and stretching in some way.

Prioritize the list and then open the door!

Blending Work and Passion

Have a Passion Breakfast for all employees, a team, or one-on-one. Ask, "What do you love to do?" "At work?" "Outside of work?" Brainstorm and commit to helping them build more of what they love into their workday.

An Exception to the Rules

Give a Bend the Rules pass that involves and encourages going against the status quo. Bend as much as possible when employees make their requests.

Genie in a Bottle

Ask an employee to write down six ways he or she would like to be rewarded. Anything goes. The only rule is that half of the ideas have to be low or no cost.

A Chance to Download

Give 12 coupons for listening time—one for each month, in which an employee can talk about anything for 20 minutes. Your job is not to understand, just to listen.

Honoring Values

Over a cappuccino, glass of wine, or cup of tea, ask an employee any of these questions:

- What do you think makes a perfect day at work?
- Looking back, what has satisfied you the most?
- What does the word "success" mean to you?

Take notes and read them back to the employee, discussing his or her values.

The Starring Role, For Once

Give an employee a chance to lead a project. Offer the spotlight, yield, coach when necessary.

Performance

Employees want to be recognized for the jobs they were hired to do. The most effective incentives are based on job performance—not on nonperformance-related praise, such as attendance or attire.

These influences should be considered when integrating motivation into job design, performance feedback, pay-for-performance systems, and relationship-building initiatives.

J.R. Hackman and G.R. Oldham's job characteristics model explains in detail how managers can make jobs more interesting and motivating for employees.

According to Hackman and Oldham (Lauby 2005), every job has five characteristics that determine how motivated workers will find that job. These characteristics determine how employees react to their work and lead to such outcomes as high performance and satisfaction, and low absenteeism and turnover.

1. Skill Variety

The extent to which a job requires an employee to use a wide range of skills, abilities, or knowledge is referred to as skill variety. For example, the skill variety required by the job of a research scientist is higher than that required by the job of a food server.

2. Task Identity

Task identity refers to the extent to which a job requires a worker to perform all of the tasks necessary to complete that job from the beginning to the end of the production process. For example, a crafts worker who takes a piece of wood and transforms it into a custom-made piece of furniture, such as a desk, has higher task identity than a worker who performs only one of the numerous operations required to assemble a television.

3. Task Significance

The degree to which a worker feels his or her job is meaningful because of its effect on people inside the organization (such as co-workers) or to people outside the organization (such as customers) is task significance. A teacher who sees the effect of his or her efforts in a well-educated and well-adjusted student enjoys high task significance compared with a dishwasher who monotonously washes dishes as they come into the kitchen.

4. Autonomy

Autonomy refers to the degree to which a job gives an employee the freedom and discretion needed to schedule different tasks and to decide how to carry out those tasks. Salespeople who have to plan their schedules and decide how to allocate their time among different customers have relatively high autonomy compared with assembly-line workers whose actions are determined by the speed of the production line.

5. Feedback

The extent to which performing a job provides a worker with clear and direct information about how well he or she has completed the job is feedback.

Hackman and Oldham (Lauby 2005) argue that these five characteristics influence an employee's motivation because they affect three critical psychological states. If employees feel that their work is meaningful and that they are responsible for work outcomes and for knowing how those outcomes affect others, the employees will find the work more motivating, be more satisfied, and thus perform at a high level.

Three Change States

Change is a process that must be carefully orchestrated at each level of the organization. There are three states to a change process: current state, transition state, and future state. To move from the current state to the future state, targets of change must pass through a transition state, a period of high insecurity and ambiguity in which people are unfrozen from their current ways of thinking and doing and are drawn into a new frame of reference.

Characteristics of a transition state include

- low stability

- high emotional stress

- high, often undirected, energy

- control as a major issue

- highly valued past patterns of behavior

- increased conflict.

Managers must understand and address these characteristics to maintain employee motivation to see the change state through to the desired state.

Retention and Longevity Studies

Employee turnover is an important issue. Highlighting the basic distinctions involved in retention, turnover, and so forth will help clarify these topics:

- Retention relates to the percentage of employees remaining in the organization. High levels of retention are desired in most job groups.

- Turnover is the opposite of retention and refers to the percentage of employees leaving the organization for any reason.

- Turnover rate refers to the rate at which individuals leave.

- Tenure is the length of time an individual is employed by the organization and is usually related to the concept of employee loyalty. A loyal employee usually remains with an organization for a long period of time. In many organizations, it is desirable to have long-tenured employees, although this situation taken to an extreme can also create problems.

Becoming an employer of choice often involves acquiring the best talent for the organization, motivating employees to improve performance, keeping them satisfied and loyal, developing them so they can grow and contribute skills, and ultimately retaining them (Fitz-enz 2000).

Rewards

Although money, according to Nelson (1994), is important to employees, what tends to motivate them to perform—and to perform at higher levels—is the thoughtful, personal kind of recognition that signifies true appreciation for a job well done. In addition, motivation for self-actualized individuals lies in the number and type of opportunities for growth and achievement their work provides. These motivational strategies are adapted from Nelson:

- Make a thank-you card by hand.

- Buy an employee lunch as a form of thanks or to mark a special event.

- Greet employees by name when you see them.

- Engrave a plaque with the names of employees who have served five, 10, and 20 years.

- Give the person more autonomy.

- Pay membership dues for a professional association.

- Create symbols of a team's work such as T-shirts or coffee mugs with a motto or logo.

- Give higher-performing employees the chance to telecommute.

- Encourage employee suggestions, and reward those whose suggestions are implemented.

Role of Empowered Employees

Most organizations boast of their goals for employee development and growth. Managers, supervisors, and employees need to discuss and agree on the methods that will be used before development and growth will occur. The change process should be defined to include the direction and benefits of the change.

Supervisors and employees can support management's desire for change by individual work assignments. In most cases, individuals know that they want change but may be unable to articulate exactly how and where they would like the change to occur. A system that recognizes this flaw can be successful by allowing the individual to clarify what type of work satisfies him or her and his or her personal values as compared with the characteristics of the job. With this method, change is desirable and positive.

The Basics of Effective Rewards

Although money is an important motivator, employees value recognition of a job well done more than anything. These are characteristics of effective rewards:

Immediate

Delay will seriously affect the effectiveness of any reward. Managers should be sure to thank employees right away for good performance and provide any tangible awards as soon as possible.

Sincere

Managers should not praise employees if they do not mean it. Insincere praise does more harm than good, both to the employee involved and to others who will discount any praise—sincere or not—that they get in the future.

Specific

Generalizations give employees the idea that managers do not even know what they do. By including the details of the employees' accomplishments, managers can let employees know that they value and pay attention to employees' achievements.

> **Positive**
>
> Managers should only discuss the positive aspects of an employee's performance when recognizing his or her achievements. Any hint of criticism will undermine the motivational effort. Ways an employee could improve his or her performance should be discussed at another time.
>
> Source: Adapted from Nelson (1994).

Value of Internal Change Agents at All Levels

The vast majority of the time, the key issues, resources, and performers fall outside the authority of a change manager. Therefore, partnering is a critical aspect of any change initiative. It is crucial to work with all employees affected by change to design collaborative approaches. It is, therefore, necessary to identify key players (such as those who own key resources that are needed as well as the top performers) and work with them.

Effective partnering requires the ability to negotiate expectations and roles upfront. In addition, good diplomacy to build alliances and gain access to important resources is critical. Finally, insight into change management issues aids the partnering issue.

It's important to manage expectations and guide employees in the right direction. It's also necessary to identify if the change initiative involves diagnostic analysis (dealing with poor performance) or new performance planning (current performance is fine, but improvement is desired, perhaps because business goals are being raised or new types of work will be done).

Partnering must continue throughout the entire change process. It is important to partner during the initiative design phase, pulling in key resources from other departments. Partnering is also critical during the roll-out effort, which likely will include a communication plan and a series of ways for reaching out to participants of projects that involve large numbers of performers.

Action Steps for Overcoming Resistance to Change

If managers are not getting the motivational mileage that they should as managers, perhaps they are making one of the following five management mistakes.

Misplacing Ownership

Many think motivation is the job of the human resources (HR) department. Although many companies give their HR departments some responsibility for formal rewards and recognition programs, that doesn't mean managers are off the hook. In many situations, employees find that informal recognition from their managers for a job well done means more to them than a formal company program.

Misaligning Incentives

It is a mistake to give each employee the same incentive. No single action will motivate all employees. It's a manager's job to determine the unique motivators for each employee and to provide an appropriate motivator when recognition is deserved.

Saving Recognition

It's inappropriate to save recognition for special occasions. When employees perform at a high level, managers should recognize that success—regularly and often.

Playing Favorites

Managers should neither give handouts nor play favorites. They should not give recognition when none is warranted. That act not only cheapens the value of the incentive but also makes a manager lose credibility. In interactions with employees, credibility is one of the most important qualities that a manager can build. Lose that, and managers could lose everything.

Misspeaking Praise

When praising employees, do not just say, "Good job." Be specific so that employees know exactly what they did to receive recognition. This simple act—providing detailed praise—helps to develop the skills and abilities of the workforce.

The mind is a muscle. If the minds of employees go unchallenged, they will start to atrophy. The workforce is full of creative people ready for an interesting, invigorating challenge. If an organization wants to keep its top performers, new projects or opportunities must be created for them.

Motivating Learners

How often do people question the ways in which other people perceive and process information? Whether with frustration, amusement, or acceptance, adults realize that working with people means dealing with their distinct information-handling styles. Different habits and points of view shape learning styles, which, as psychologist David Kolb (1984) has pointed out in **Kolb's learning style inventory**, are closely tied to problem-tackling and problem-solving styles for getting along in life. It is true: Adults live and learn how to cope.

A trainer may have a chance, through administration of learning style assessment instruments, to predetermine learners' styles and, perhaps, to group training participants according to results. But this is usually not possible. By being aware of the strengths and weaknesses of different training and learning styles and methods, a trainer can

- take an important step toward improved communication with learners who do not share the trainer's style tendencies and preferences

- build on the strengths of his or her own training style

- do a better job of designing, developing, and delivering training that accommodates learners' individual needs.

Awareness of Potential Cultural Differences

As people grow up in their homes, communities, and nations, they get and react to expressed and tacit signals about how to process information. For example, as children, some have had these experiences:

- Adults may have provided too much encouragement to touch and manipulate things, to ask questions, and to express opinions. Or they may have said to be quiet and leave everything alone.

- Some people may or may not have seen neighborhood adults—at work or for pleasure—often reading or working with their hands. Others may or may not have seen women or minority group members in positions of authority.

- Some may have enjoyed school activities and the approval of classmates and teachers. Or some may have felt confused or left out.

Adult learners have various histories of formal education and training. An adult might say "I learned my lesson" though a life experience. What is interesting is that the same life lesson may lead different people to different conclusions. A failure causes one person to give up; a second to redouble efforts; and a third to reflect, change in some way, then try again, and so on. As individuals, each may be making a rational, valid choice or may be reacting to the emotional aftermath of an earlier, perceived failure.

Everyone differs in his or her personalities, feelings, values, biases, preferences, and expectations. Some "walk with personality, talk with personality," and may "have a great big smile." These characteristics also affect ways of learning and motivation to learn.

Learning Styles

There are a number of instruments that address the various ways learners process and organize information. One of these is the Kolb learning style inventory. Developed by David Kolb (1984), these are part of his work in experiential learning—which he describes as an "integrative perspective . . . that combines experience, perception, cognition, and behavior." His impressive body of research relates learning styles to

- Jung's personality types

- educational specialization

- careers and jobs

- adaptive consequences.

Kolb (1984) has written about learners' orientation to four learning modes: concrete experience, reflective observation, abstract conceptualization, and active experimentation

Figure 11-1. Kolb's Learning Styles

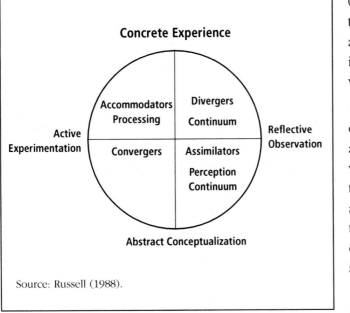

Concrete Experience

Accommodators Processing | Divergers Continuum

Active Experimentation | Reflective Observation

Convergers | Assimilators Perception Continuum

Abstract Conceptualization

Source: Russell (1988).

(see figure 11-1). Each orientation is explained in this section, along with the training style that is most appropriate for working with these learners:

- *Concrete experience:* This orientation "emphasizes feeling as opposed to thinking." People with this orientation take an "artistic" approach. They are intuitive and open-minded and do well in the absence of structure. Trainers of people with this orientation should function as motivators.

- *Reflective observation:* This orientation involves "understanding the meaning of ideas and situations by carefully observing and impartially describing them." People with this orientation can see the implications of different approaches and are good at understanding different points of view. Instructors of people with this orientation should function as experts.

- *Abstract conceptualization:* This orientation concentrates on "thinking as opposed to feeling." People with this orientation like to take a scientific, systematic approach and enjoy working with symbols and analyzing information to formulate general theories. Their trainers should serve as coaches, providing guided practice and feedback.

- *Active experimentation:* This orientation "focuses on actively influencing people and changing situations . . . [and] emphasizes practical applications." People with this orientation like to get things done. Instructors of these people should stay out of the way, providing them maximum opportunities to discover for themselves.

Kolb asserts that the key to effective learning is being competent in each mode when it is appropriate. Kolb's learning style inventory identifies a person's learning style according to the quadrants between pairs of modes, and Kolb's learning style inventory is scored and plotted to indicate where within a quadrant a person's responses fall. Kolb categorizes learners and their respective "adaptive competencies" as follows:

- *Convergers:* These people do best with one-right-answer tests and situations. They are strong in resolving technical problems but do not fare as well in interpersonal dealings. They are decisive, experiment with new possibilities, and set goals.

- *Divergers:* These people are imaginative and sensitive to meanings, values, and feelings. They keep an open mind, gather information, and can envision the implications of situations and choices.

- *Assimilators:* These people are good at creating abstract models. They organize information, test theories, design tests and experiments, analyze quantitative information, and can construct conceptual models.

- *Accommodators:* These people take risks, adapt to circumstances, and take action. They often work by trial and error, depend on other people for analysis of information, and may be viewed as impatient by the more contemplative types. They look for and use opportunities, are involved and committed, and can work well with, or lead, other people.

Diversity Guidelines

Diversity training has expanded over the years to include developing skills that enhance productivity and communication organization-wide. Negative stereotypes may be overcome through team building exercises in which team members of different backgrounds increase the frequency and quality of their interactions.

The world of work does not look the same as it did 50 years ago. The workforce is significantly different, as are customers. It will look even more diverse 10 years from now. To ensure that all employees feel respected and appreciated, recognizing the talents of each person in the organization is important. Recognizing the value of diversity is important from an individual perspective and from an organizational perspective. Individual contributors are motivated by inclusion, making a difference, achievement, and recognition, whereas organizations are motivated by making a profit, which is easier to do with teams working smoothly and in harmony. Businesses also want to reduce expenses, including dollars spent as a result of miscommunication, legal fees, turnover, repeated training, and grievances. Together, everyone's goals can be reached by working toward the same clear purpose and practicing values that support the respect and dignity of all those partnering to achieve success.

✓ **Chapter 11 Knowledge Check**

1. **According to various studies, monetary rewards are the highest motivators in reward systems.**

    __ **A.** True

    ✓ **B.** False

2. **Which of the following is *not* an example of a motivational strategy?**

    __ **A.** Making a homemade thank-you card

    __ **B.** Giving an employee more autonomy

    ✓ **C.** Tapping into an employee's trust network

    __ **D.** Creating symbols of a team's work with a motto or logo

3. **Partnering is a critical aspect of any change initiative.**

    ✓ **A.** True

    __ **B.** False

4. **During organizational change, employees may need new information or skills. Who created the learning style inventory about learner's orientation to four learning modes: concrete experience, reflective observation, abstract conceptualization, and active experimentation?**

    __ **A.** Knowles

    __ **B.** Junt

    ✓ **C.** Kolb

    __ **D.** Herzberg

5. **Which of the following learning style orientations is best described as "feeling as opposed to thinking"?**

    ✓ **A.** Concrete experience

    __ **B.** Reflective observation

    __ **C.** Abstract conceptualization

    __ **D.** Active experimentation

6. **During an organizational change, employees must move from the present state to the desired state. During this process, targets of change must go through a transition state. Which of the following is *not* a characteristic associated with this transition state when an organizational change occurs?**

__ **A.** Low, often undirected, energy

__ **B.** Control as a major issue

__ **C.** Low stability

__ **D.** Increased conflict

7. **When developing a reward system, rewards need to have specific characteristics. Which of the following is *not* one of the characteristics that a reward should include?**

__ **A.** Rewards need to be specific to indicate that the manager values and pays attention to achievements.

__ **B.** Rewards should always have a tangible value.

__ **C.** Rewards should include sincere praise.

__ **D.** Rewards are time sensitive and immediate.

References

Cowan, S.L. (1999). "Change Management." *Infoline* No. 259904.

Darraugh, B., editor. (1991). "How to Motivate Employees." *Infoline* No. 259108.

Fitz-enz, J. (2000). *The ROI of Human Capital: Measuring the Economic Value of Employee Performance*. New York: AMACOM.

Kamine, M., C. de Mello-e-Souza Wildermuth, and R. Collins. (2003). "Diversity Programs That Work." *Infoline* No. 250312.

Kaye, B.L., and S. Jordan-Evans. (December 2000). "The ABCs of Management Gift-Giving." *T&D*, pp. 51–54.

Kolb, D.A. (1984). *Experiential Learning: Experience as the Source of Learning and Development*. Englewood Cliffs, NJ: Prentice-Hall.

Lauby, S. (2005). "Motivating Employees." *Infoline* No. 250510.

Nelson, B. (1994). *1001 Ways to Reward Employees*. New York: Workman Publishing.

Phillips, J.J., editor. (2002). *In Action: Retaining Your Best Employees*. Alexandria, VA: ASTD Press.

Russell, S. (1998). "Training and Learning Styles." *Infoline* No. 258804.

Smith, W. (1989). "Managing Change: Implementation Skills." *Infoline* No. 258910. (Out of print.)

12
Mindset and Mental Models

Each workplace learning and performance professional brings his or her own unique knowledge, skills, and experience to the workplace. Deep-seated assumptions about human performance are often challenged and require expanded thinking to accept new ideas, tools, and processes. Consistent mindfulness, awareness, and willingness to change styles are required to be successful.

Learning Objectives:

- ☑ List and describe common management styles.
- ☑ Explain how personal social styles can affect change.
- ☑ Define *emotional intelligence* and its effect on change.

Management Styles

There are nearly as many distinct management styles as there are managers; however, to simplify this topic, here are some basic definitions for some very general management styles:

- *Dictatorship:* Authoritarian style of management; military chain of command type structure. The manager takes complete control of work without regard to input from employees and expects total obedience.

- *Anarchy:* Employees work with no input from managers. Work processes are dependent on employees.

- *Democracy:* Most popular form of management in most organizations; allows for sharing of ideas among employees and managers. Managers look for feedback. Equality is valued, and employees have a sense of investment in the organization.

According to "Pygmalion in Management" by Sterling Livingston (2002): "Some managers always treat their subordinates in a way that leads to superior performance. But most managers, such as Professor Higgins [in 'Pygmalion'] unintentionally treat their subordinates in a way that leads to lower performance than they are capable of achieving. The way managers treat their subordinates is subtly influenced by what they expect of them." Therefore, the assumption for this section is that the three styles listed previously (dictatorship, anarchy, democracy) occur as a result of managers' own mindsets, and that those mindsets have a direct effect on employee productivity

Personal Social Styles

A person's social style has a direct effect on his or her ability to learn and change. Harvey A. Robbins, in *How to Speak and Listen Effectively* (1992), suggests that listeners come in four behavioral styles:

1. Analytical people tend toward perfectionism and deal in logic and details. They tend to keep feelings to themselves. In talking with them, preparing the case in advance and being accurate and realistic is helpful. It is important to provide tangible evidence to support major points.

2. Amiable people put a high value on people and friendships. They go out of their way not to offend. They have opinions but are not inclined to say what's on their mind. To draw out their opinions, asking "how" questions is a good tactic.

3. Drivers can appear to be pushy at times, making demands on themselves and others. They tend to keep emotions under wraps and resent those who gossip and waste time in idle conversation. They are decisive and results-oriented and like to give guidance to those who need it and those who do not as well. When dealing with drivers, people should be brief, specific, and to the point.

4. Expressive people are looking for a good time. They are enthusiastic, creative, and intuitive but have little tolerance for those unlike themselves. Easily bored, they tend to go off on tangents. When dealing with this type, it's useful to stick with the big picture.

For more information, see Module 2, *Delivering Training*, chapter 8, "Individual Learning Styles."

Emotional Intelligence

Emotional intelligence can be defined in many ways, but on the most basic level, it is the ability to accurately identify and understand a person's own emotional reactions and those of others. It also involves the ability to regulate a person's own emotions, to use them to make good decisions, and to act effectively (Mayer, Salovey, and Caruso 1998). Emotional intelligence is the basis for personal qualities, such as realistic self-confidence, personal integrity, knowledge of personal strengths and weaknesses, resilience in times of change or adversity, self-motivation, perseverance, and the knack for getting along well with others.

People with intrapersonal intelligence know themselves. They are aware of their strengths and weaknesses, desires and fears, joys and sorrows. They use that knowledge to adapt positively to changing circumstances, a behavioral characteristic known as resiliency. Interpersonal intelligence describes how individuals know and understand others, particularly at the level of feeling and emotional response. People with interpersonal intelligence are sensitive to others, notice their emotional cues, and respond appropriately to help others feel safe and cared about. As those two intelligences come together, the end result is a person who works effectively with many types of individuals. In fact, the hallmark of emotionally intelligent people is that they make others feel good to be around them. Their ways of interacting are inevitably encouraging, supportive, and helpful.

As they look toward the future, organizations can anticipate that customer needs and wants will change. To meet those unknown and evolving expectations, organizations will need to build teams of diverse specialists who can form powerful work groups and produce results. Those who do so will innovate, produce new products and services, and help shape the developing industries of tomorrow. Available evidence supports the fact that increasing emotional intelligence produces more effective work groups; greater harmony in the workplace; and, ultimately, more resilient organizations.

✓ Chapter 12 Knowledge Check

1. The following are the most common management styles *except*

   __ **A.** Anarchy

   __ **B.** Democracy

   __ **C.** Dictatorship

   _ **D.** Diplomacy

2. Which management style is most appropriately defined as employees working with no input from management and the processes are dependent on employees?

   _ **A.** Anarchy

   __ **B.** Democracy

   __ **C.** Dictatorship

   __ **D.** Diplomacy

3. A training manager calls a meeting to discuss strategies for the next fiscal year. She begins the meeting by setting the tone of the discussion and then asks for feedback around her ideas and any other ideas her team might have. This type of management style is best described as a _____ management style.

   _ **A.** Democratic

   __ **B.** Interactive

   __ **C.** Diplomatic

   __ **D.** Productive

4. All of the following are types of social styles *except*

   __ **A.** Amiable

   __ **B.** Analytical

   __ **C.** Driver

   _ **D.** Emotional

5. People with this social style are often perfectionists who deal in logic and details and tend to keep feelings to themselves.

   __ **A.** Amiable

   _ **B.** Analytical

   __ **C.** Driver

   __ **D.** Emotional

6. **A person's social style has a direct effect on his or her ability to learn and change.**

   _ **A.** True

   _ **B.** False

7. **A WLP professional barks out orders to a fellow teammate and is highly demanding of himself and others. When dealing with this person, one should do all of the following *except***

   _ **A.** Provide thorough examples

   _ **B.** Be specific

   _ **C.** Be brief

   _ **D.** Make your point quickly

8. **A WLP professional is characterized by many on her team as someone who is constantly making work fun. She is enthusiastic and engaged but sometimes finds herself bored and disconnected when others go off on tangents on a particular topic. This WLP professional's personal style can best be described as**

   _ **A.** Amiable

   _ **B.** Analytical

   _ **C.** Driver

   _ **D.** Expressive

9. **Employing emotionally intelligent people leads to greater resilience in times of change or adversity.**

   _ **A.** True

   _ **B.** False

References

Cherniss, C., and M. Adler. (2000). *Promoting Emotional Intelligence in Organizations.* Alexandria, VA: ASTD Press.

Kirrane, D. (1988). "Listening to Learn: Learning to Listen." *Infoline* No. 258806. (Out of print.)

Livingston, J.S. (September 2002). "Pygmalion in Management." *Harvard Business Review,* pp. 81–89.

Mayer, J.D., P. Salovey, and D. Caruso. (1998). "Competing Models of Emotional Intelligence." *Handbook of Human Intelligence,* R.J. Steinberg, editor. New York: Cambridge University Press.

Robbins, H.A. (1992). *How to Speak and Listen Effectively.* New York: AMACOM.

Appendix A
Glossary

4-D Cycle is the approach used in appreciative inquiry consisting of four phases: discovery, dream, design, destiny.

Action Research and learning is both a model and a process. In its simplest form, it is a process whereby research or fact-finding precedes action and follows it. The thought process looks something like this: fact-finding, action, fact-finding, action, and so on. The action research process takes shape as understanding increases. The process remains focused on the desired state and how each systemic element needs to change.

Appreciative Inquiry Theory is an approach to large-scale organizational change that involves the analysis of positive and successful (rather than negative or failing) operations. The appreciative inquiry 4-D cycle (discovery, dream, design, destiny) includes identifying problems, analyzing causes, searching for solutions, and developing an action plan.

Chaos is the study of how simple systems can generate complicated behavior.

Chaos and Complexity Theory is a scientific theory that is applied to organization development in an attempt to find order in the organizational environment.

Closed-Ended, or direct, questions help to check for understanding or to test for consensus. These are sometimes preferable to open-ended questions to limit information.

Complex Systems have details, whose role in the larger system cannot be understood fully by examining them apart from the system. By carefully studying the whole system, patterns can be identified.

Complexity is the study of how complicated systems generate simple behavior.

Confirmative Evaluation provides the intermediate and long-term information to demonstrate that the desired future state is occurring. Continuing results are measured against expected results.

Discovery Learning is the process of teaching participants by having them actively engage in the activity to learn it.

Emotional Intelligence is an "eighth intelligence" based on Gardner's multiple intelligence theory, which suggests an ability to accurately identify and understand one's own emotional reactions and those of others and is related to personal qualities, such as self-confidence and motivation. The theory was developed by Daniel Goleman in the 1990s and popularized in his book, *Emotional Intelligence*.

Experiential Learning occurs when a learner participates in an activity, reviews the activity, identifies useful knowledge or skills that were gained, and transfers the result to the workplace.

Experiential Learning Activities (ELAs) are part of the experiential learning cycle that explains what must occur during an activity to ensure maximum learning occurs. The five steps are: experiencing, publishing, processing, generalizing, and applying.

Flat Management Model is a model in which the line of authority flows from the top to the lower levels of the organization. On each level, managers have authority over their areas (for example, credit and human resources managers) and subordinates, who, in turn, have authority over others, and so on. Every employee reports to a single immediate superior.

Forcefield Analysis is a diagnostic tool developed by Kurt Lewin to assess two types of forces related to introducing change in organizations: driving and restraining. Driving forces are those that help implement the change, whereas restraining forces are those that will get in the way of the change.

Formative Evaluation begins with performance analysis—questioning whether the methods used are best for this effort, the right people are involved, the right data analysis tools are used, and so on.

Intervention is another name for a solution or set of solutions, usually a combination of tools and techniques that clearly and directly relate to solving a performance gap.

Kepner-Tregoe describes a practical, straightforward decision-making process by dividing criteria into musts and wants. The musts are definable into either/or categories. The wants are those relative measures that are important but cannot be quantified into yes or no answers.

Kolb's Learning Style Inventory developed by David Kolb, is an inventory of four learning styles or modes (concrete experience, reflective observation, abstract conceptualization, and active experimentation) and individuals' orientation to them. Kolb categorizes learners as convergers, divergers, assimilators, or accommodators.

Leadership Development focuses on learning events, such as mentoring, training, self-study, and job rotations to prepare employees with the skills required to lead an organization.

Learning Style describes an individual's approach to learning that involves the way he or she behaves, feels, and processes information.

Matrix Model is a model of management that is a combination line and project structure with a general manager at the top of the hierarchy. The purpose of matrix structures is to integrate diverse areas of expertise.

Motivation Theory is based on the idea that by creating the right environment for people to work in, they will be motivated to grow and become connected to that environment. This theory is important to coaching.

Open Systems Theory, also known as living or general systems theory, is based on the idea that things influence each other, or that groups of people (in an organization) learn from one another.

Open-Ended questions stimulate discussion. Open-ended questions have no one specific correct answer and encourage individuals to draw on their own experiences and apply them to the current situation or discussion.

Organizational Culture is the unspoken pattern of values that guide the behavior of the people in an organization, including attitudes and practices that can be difficult to change.

Organization Development (OD) is the process of developing an organization to be more effective in achieving its business goals. OD uses planned initiatives to develop the systems, structures, and process within the organization to improve effectiveness.

Provocative Proposition is a statement that bridges the best of "what is" with speculation or intuition of "what might be." It is provocative to the extent to which it stretches the realm of the status quo, challenges common assumptions or routines, and helps suggest real possibilities that represent desired possibilities for the organization and its people.

Return-on-Investment (ROI) is a ratio of the benefit or profit received from a given investment to the cost of the investment itself. It constitutes accountability for training programs.

Sender-Receiver Model postulates that communication between two people goes through each person's filters.

Six Sigma Methodology is a process-improvement strategy and measure of quality that strives for near perfection. Six Sigma is a disciplined, data-driven methodology for eliminating defects (driving toward six standard deviations between the mean and the nearest specification limit) in a process. The fundamental objective of the Six Sigma methodology is the implementation of a measurement-based strategy that focuses on process improvement and variation reduction through the application to projects.

Summative Evaluation begins to summarize results based on immediate reaction of initiative implementation.

Systems Thinking is a conceptual framework that encompasses the whole, making patterns (and ways to change them) more understandable.

Theory X is the traditional way of looking at the workforce, an approach that assumes that people would rather play than work.

Theory Y postulates that most people will work to achieve goals to which they are committed, especially if rewards result from the achievement of those objectives and that most people can learn to accept—and even seek—responsibility.

Appendix B
Answer Key

Chapter 1

1. Employing systems thinking allows an organization to assess a situation holistically and determine where to make the most effective intervention.

A. True

Response A is correct because systems thinking involves looking at issues from a holistic perspective and determining what underlying, fundamental relationships are contributing to the issue. This enables organizations to determine the best place to make any changes.

2. The management team of a manufacturing firm is constantly reacting to new problems and does not seem to have the time to make long-range plans. The management team needs to apply a systems thinking approach because

C. It will allow the management team to uncover the root causes contributing to the problems and consider the effect of any implemented changes

Response C is correct because systems thinking allows the team to consider how changes in one area of the organization will affect other areas of the organization, thereby enabling the team to understand the effects of small changes and avoid the occurrence of major problems.

3. Which of the following recognizes the interrelationships of the parts and the importance of their interaction to create the whole?

B. Systems view

Response B is correct because a systems view is a perspective of the whole that takes into account everything that makes up the whole and how those parts interact. It's a way to keep the bigger picture in mind while collecting data and information about an organization.

4. One of the benefits of systems thinking is the ability to discern patterns of recurring problems not driven by daily events.

A. True

Response A is correct because systems thinking enables practitioners to look at problems by taking a longer-term view that may not be affected by daily occurrences.

5. Which of the following is *not* one of the three perspectives on problems?

C. Resources

Response C is the correct because it is not a level to view problems in this model. Resources may be a potential source of the problems.

6. Which of the following is *not* a characteristic of a systems thinker?

B. Focuses on independent, mutually exclusive relationships

Response B is correct because focusing on independent, mutually exclusive relationships is not a characteristic of a systems thinker. On the contrary, systems thinkers engage stakeholders, consider multiple perspectives, and create a shared understanding of problems.

7. Which of the following is *not* a principle of systems thinking?

A. Solutions should be decided and implemented as quickly as possible.

Response A is correct because the idea that solutions should be decided and implemented as quickly as possible is not a principle of systems thinking. It contravenes the longer-term and more fundamental approach to problem solving that is characteristic of systems thinking.

8. The chief learning officer (CLO) of a consulting firm needs to recruit a training director with strong systems thinking capabilities. In preparation for the interview, the CLO is compiling a list of needed skills. In reviewing the candidates' references, one candidate's description should eliminate this candidate from the pool because this characteristic is not indicative of a systems thinker. Which candidate should be eliminated?

B. Candidate B. In making decisions responds quickly and decisively to unforeseen events as they arise

Response B is correct because responding decisively to events may be necessary for a systems thinker at times, but generally speaking, a systems thinker works to avoid the need to respond quickly to events

by being proactive in eliminating emergency situations.

9. Which of the following theories postulates the view that any organization is a system that absorbs such environmental inputs as people factors, raw materials, capital, and information; uses them in such transformational processes as service delivery or manufacturing methods; and expels them as outputs, such as finished goods or customer services?

C. Open systems theory

Response C is correct because open systems theory views organizations as systems through which external inputs are transformed into value-added outputs, such as products and services.

10. Open systems theory examines

A. Inputs/outputs and external/internal relationships

Response A is correct because open systems theory examines the organization as a system that absorbs environmental inputs and uses them to create output. It looks at the internal and external factors and their interrelationships to understand the influences on the organization.

Chapter 2

1. Which of the following terms is most appropriately defined as the study of how simple systems can generate complicated behavior and is a state where patterns cannot be made nor details understood?

B. Chaos

Response B is correct because chaos is a confused, disorganized state in which behavior becomes unpredictable. This confusion makes it difficult to discern patterns or understand details.

2. Which of the following states that the central premise as it relates to organizations is that order can emerge out of chaos?

A. Complexity

Response A is correct because complexity refers to a state of multiple, interrelated parts in which patterns can be discerned. For this reason, a complex situation is initially chaotic, but with the difference that order can be imposed upon it.

3. Which of the following is *not* an example of the pros of using the chaos and complexity theory?

B. Rigidity

Response B is correct because it is not an advantage of using chaos and complexity theory. On the contrary, using chaos and complexity allows a great deal of flexibility by creating a culture that enables organizations to respond rapidly to change.

4. Which of the following encourages a holistic approach so that changes or initiatives in one component of an organization do not negatively affect another part of the organization?

D. Systems thinking

Response D is correct because systems thinking looks at the ramifications of all decisions and changes. Because systems are made up of interrelated parts, a small change in one place can have unintended consequences in other areas. Systems thinking enables practitioners to predict areas where a change may have an effect. Response A is incorrect because system archetypes are generic system configurations that can be applied to many situations.

5. Which of the following best describes how the chaos theory relates to organizational change?

C. Chaos is the result of an organizational system resisting change and then reaching a point where change is unavoidable. At this point, change occurs rapidly and can take the system into unexpected directions.

Response C is correct because complex systems like organizations are stable and thus resist change. As the pressure of change builds up on the system, it eventually gives way, throwing the system into chaotic imbalance.

6. Although theorists do not agree on which characteristics are most important with regard to chaotic and complex systems, most accept several characteristics as the central part of the chaos and complexity theory. These characteristics include all *but which* of the following?

A. Problem events within a system are usually microcosms of the chaos within it, and dissecting an individual event reveals the key issue of the organization.

Response A is correct because this is not a characteristic of chaos or complexity theory. One of the key elements of chaos and complexity theory is the examination of the whole. Individual isolated events do not provide enough information to provide a clear view of the organization.

7. Learning organizations accept the fact that nothing is always stable and that they must be prepared to quickly change their strategies to adapt.

A. True

Response A is correct because learning organizations practice systems thinking. An important tenet of systems thinking is that organizations evolve continually. This continual change means that nothing is stable all of the time, and the best way to deal with the threat of instability is to become adaptable.

8. Organizations creating a successful environment for change should focus on creating a vision, communicating the plan, connecting with people, and congratulating on successes.

A. True

Response A is correct because creating a vision is important to get everyone in the organization to buy in to the change. Communication is another critical component of successful change to help employees understand and accept the change, to alleviate their fears, and to understand the benefits waiting for them. Connecting with people is another way to help employees get on board with the changes as well as to learn what kinds of issues they are coming across as a result of the changes. Finally, congratulating on successes helps to keep morale high during a period of change.

9. An internal change consultant is working with the managers to agree to loosen their control and allow teams to self-organize. Which theory is the consultant using to help facilitate change in this organization?

D. Chaos and complexity theory

Response D is correct because the central premise of complexity theory is that order can emerge from chaos. Having managers create a strong sense of vision in their employees and then allowing them to create courses of action for themselves is one way to implement this theory.

10. What is the order for the four Cs of change?

C. Create, Communicate, Connect, Congratulate

Response C is correct because the WLP professional can help change to occur in organizations by first creating the vision for change, then communicating it to gain buy-in, connecting with the people in the organization as the change is occurring, then congratulating to help keep up morale and recognize successes along the way, even if they are small.

Chapter 3

1. Which of the following uses data collection in the form of collecting people's stories of something at its best by structuring questions and information to focus on the positive to initiate organizational change?

D. Appreciative inquiry theory

Response D is correct because appreciative inquiry is an approach to large-scale organizational change that involves the analysis of positive and successful (rather than negative or failing) operations, which involves collecting data in the form of people's stories.

2. Cooperrider and Srivastva developed the 4-D cycle, which includes discovery, dream, design, and deliver, to guide OD professionals and clients through the appreciative inquiry approach.

B. False

Response B is correct because, although Cooperrider and Srivastva did originate the concept of appreciative inquiry and develop the 4-D cycle, the four Ds in the cycle are discovery, dream, design, and destiny.

3. One way that OD practitioners can begin using the appreciative inquiry approach is by adding positively focused questions to their coaching, consulting, and facilitating.

A. True

Response A is correct because using positive and hopeful questions that are focused on successes and possibilities is the most common way to begin a change process that follows the appreciative inquiry approach. Rather than beginning with a full-on appreciative inquiry in an organization, OD practitioners can use this type of questioning to get practice in using the approach.

4. What phase of the 4-D cycle includes developing statements such as, "We want to be the employer of choice," "We want to delight our customers," and "We want to envision ideas for growth"?

A. Topic

Response A is correct because the outset of an appreciative inquiry process involves determining the topic that the organization will focus on. The topic should be something important to the organization and an area that, if improved, will make a big difference.

5. In what phase of the 4-D cycle do participants explore and discuss their visions, hopes, ideas, and dreams for the future?

B. Dream

Response B is correct because the dream phase of the 4-D cycle is where the members of the change team will work together to explore possibilities for the future.

6. An output of the design phase in the 4-D cycle includes powerful statements referred to as provocative propositions.

A. True

Response A is correct because the design phase is where plans are made to bring about the vision of the future through provocative propositions. Provocative propositions are statements that bridge the gap between the best of what is and the vision of what might be.

7. The 4-D cycle starts with dreams and ends with substantive changes in an organization's practices, processes, systems, and structures.

A. True

Response A is correct because appreciative inquiry creates an environment that engages and excites people by discovering their aspirations and then makes those dreams come true by changing the organization's practices, processes, systems, and structures.

8. Although it is critical for teams to identify the desired future state when planning a change initiative, individuals can often design and develop the needed solutions.

B. False

Response B is correct because, to be successful, the change process requires inclusion and participation even when designing and developing solutions.

9. What are the five steps in the Pfeiffer and Jones's experiential learning cycle?

B. Experiencing, publishing, processing, generalizing, applying

Response B is correct because the five steps in Pfeiffer and Jones experiential learning cycle are experiencing, publishing, processing, generalizing, and applying. The first step involves doing something. Next, observations are shared. Then dynamics or concepts are interpreted. These concepts are then applied to real life. Finally, effective change is planned.

10. Which of the following is *not* a characteristic of experiential learning activities?

B. They are unstructured and free form.

Response B is correct because experiential learning activities are structured; that is, they have specific steps and a process that must be followed to ensure results.

Chapter 4

1. An action learning team is a group of four to eight people who determine the appropriate solution to be implemented when organizations reengineer and go through change.

B. False

Response B is correct because an action learning team, although it does consist of four to eight people, does not determine appropriate solutions when organizations reengineer. The team examines an organizational problem that has no easily identifiable solution.

2. The key benefit of having members from different functional areas of the organization on the action learning team is to provide a multidisciplinary view and fresh perspectives and approaches.

A. True

Response A is correct because action learning teams benefit from a diverse makeup to provide a wide variety of perspectives on a problem.

3. The major difference between questions asked in action learning versus those asked in other settings is that, in action learning, questions

B. Not only seek answers but also help a group understand and think through possibilities

Response B is correct because action learning tackles problems through a process of first asking questions to clarify the exact nature of the problem, reflecting and identifying possible solutions, and only then taking action. This type of questioning allows the group to gain better understanding of the problem and defuse defensiveness.

4. Bloom's taxonomy and knowledge, skills, and attitude categories are relevant to organizational change in that any training or learning solutions related to the change need to focus on what new knowledge or skills are required for individuals to successfully perform their jobs in the new environment.

A. True

Response A is correct because when an organizational change requires training for employees, it is important to be able to state precisely what they should acquire as a result of the training to support the success of the initiative. Bloom's taxonomy allows the practitioner to specify what the learner will acquire, whether it is intellectual knowledge, psychomotor skills, or changed attitudes.

5. Which of the following is defined as a data-driven approach to analyzing and solving root causes of business problems to help organizations formulate and integrate business strategies and missions and to deal with constantly changing and increasingly complex requirements?

D. Six Sigma

Response D is correct because Six Sigma is a highly statistical quality improvement technique that ties business outputs directly to marketplace requirements.

6. Which of the following techniques is used to assist with a vendor selection process by dividing criteria into musts and wants categories and applying a weighted comparison to determine the best supplier?

C. Kepner-Tregoe

Response C is correct because Kepner-Tregoe refers to a practical, straightforward decision-making process that divides criteria into musts and wants, thereby allowing the practitioner to select suppliers based on a weighted comparison of criteria.

7. After action learning occurs, the action learning formula is expanded to include an I, making it L=P+Q+R+I. What does the I stand for?

C. Implementation

Response C is correct because after the action learning process of exploration of a problem occurs, a solution is implemented based on the outcome of the discussion.

8. Which of the following is *not* a criterion for determining if a project is appropriate for an action learning group?

D. Flexibility

Response D is correct because flexibility is not one of the four criteria for evaluating whether projects are appropriate for action learning groups.

9. Of the following, which is *not* a step to wrap up a meeting?

C. Norming

Response C is correct because norming is not a step in ending a meeting. It is a step in the Tuckman model of team development.

10. A trainer is trying to make his class of managers aware of the effect that intercultural communication can have on the organization. Which of the following statements is considered a recognized effect that the trainer should convey?

A. Traditional American values often conflict with values of other cultures.

Response A is correct because the values of both American and other cultures are unique to those cultures and they are not always in agreement. It is important to recognize this when working in intercultural settings to minimize incorrect assumptions and potential conflict.

Chapter 5

1. A new leader in an organization is exemplifying all of the skills of a leader. Which of the following is *not* one of the skills of a leader?

C. Manage and direct the work of subordinates

Response C is correct because leaders who are adept at using personality and skills possess the ability to influence people and organizations, provide direction and strategy for accomplishing goals and objectives, and inspire and motivate others to achieve the goals. Managing and directing the work of subordi-

nates is the role of a manager, whereas the role of a leader is to inspire, motivate, and set the strategic vision of where the organization needs to go.

2. A new executive in an organization has been using formal and informal channels of communication to inform employees about the values, beliefs, and vision for the future of the organization. By doing this, the executive is trying to do which of the following?

A. Apply leadership skills to influence others (followers) to accomplish an objective

Response A is correct because the key goal of a leader is to influence others (followers) to accomplish the objectives and goals of the organization. Direction of work is not what leaders do. Changing the organizational structure isn't accomplished only by communicating values, beliefs, and vision.

3. Which of the following statements is a disadvantage of flat organizational structures?

C. The interaction among workers is more frequent, so this structure depends more on personal relationships between workers and managers. Therefore, the structure can be more time-consuming to build than a hierarchical model.

Response C is correct because this is the primary disadvantage of a flat organization. All other choices are disadvantages of a matrix organization.

4. A WLP professional is talking with a new senior leadership team to identify resources to support continued leadership development in their new roles. During these discussions, the WLP professional discovers that the leadership team believes most people need to be highly supervised and at times coerced to do a good job. Which of the following theories does this group subscribe to?

A. Theory X

Response A is correct because McGregor's Theory X is an industrial leadership theory that postulates most people do not like to work and will avoid it when they can; that they need to be coerced, controlled, or threatened to persuade them to work; and that most people want to be told what to do and avoid responsibility.

5. A leader is reading about exceptional leaders in history and believes that these leaders were born with inherited traits suited for leadership. His thinking is most closely aligned with which leadership theory?

B. Trait theory

Response B is correct because the Trait theory arose from the Great Man/Woman theory as a way of identifying the characteristics of successful leaders. Trait theory doesn't assume that great leaders are only born, but that they are born with inherited "traits" that are particularly suited for leadership. By discovering and studying these traits, it is believed that others could become great leaders as well.

6. A key tenet of postindustrial leadership theory is

C. It is everyone's job to learn continually because leadership is demanded at every level of the organization.

Response C is correct because all other tenets listed are aligned with industrial leadership models. Postindustrial leadership models recognize a key distinction between leadership and management. These models also recognize the complexity in today's work environment and that it is everyone's role to continually learn.

7. In industrial leadership models, leadership was congruent with which of the following?

A. Hierarchies/bureaucracies with one leader at the top

Response A is correct because all other items are characteristics of postindustrial (modern) leadership models and thinking. Industrial (early) leadership models and thinking focused on one person at the top (the leader) who was the most important person to learn and make decisions.

8. A WLP professional is researching leadership models focused on people and the process of leadership where there is a key demarcation between leadership and management. All of the following postindustrial leadership models support this distinction *except*

C. Group

Response C is correct because Group theory does not describe a leadership model, and the group approach to leadership is the process by which an individual takes initiative to assist a group to move toward goal achievement in a given situation and, therefore, does not show strong demarcation between leadership and management.

9. A CEO often communicates the importance of "stretch goals," which are challenge goals that encourage employees and show confidence in their abilities to hit these goals. This CEO's leadership style is best described as

B. Achievement-oriented

Response B is correct because the achievement-oriented leadership style is characterized by leaders who set challenging goals and encourage high performance as a means of showing confidence in a group's ability.

10. An organization is facing a major leadership deficit because approximately 30 percent of the senior managers are expected to retire over the next five years. When looking at potential leaders in the organization, the current senior leaders complain that younger employees do not have the same work ethic to be willing to work 12– to 14-hour days and come into the office on weekends. The force of change affecting the organization in this case is best described as

D. Diversity in workforce across generations

Response D is correct because one of the leading forces of change in organizations today is increased diversity in the workforce with regard to gender, age, culture, and race. In this example, diversity across generations is a significant force of change for organizations because the baby boomers, the largest workforce in history, are getting ready to retire and have significantly different values from Generations X and Y.

11. All of the following are internal factors that contribute to a learning culture in an organization *except*

C. Competing for scarce resources

Response C is correct because it is the only internal factor that does not contribute to a learning culture. The other responses are all internal factors that contribute to a learning culture.

12. In which organizational model does the line of authority flow from the top to the lower levels of the organization, and, on each level, managers have authority over their areas and subordinates, who, in turn, have authority over others? In this structure, every employee reports to a single immediate supervisor.

A. Hierarchical

Response A is correct because hierarchical management models are characterized by successive layers of authority. In each layer of authority, employees report to only one boss, who has authority over his or her employees and in turn reports to only one boss and so on.

13. Which organizational structure's advantages include the following characteristics: the structure is simple and easy to comprehend, management authority and job responsibility is easily defined, and budgeting and cost controls are easier to manage?

B. Hierarchical

Response B is correct because a hierarchical structure (bureaucracy or traditional structure) has one leader at the top, with a clear manager and reporting relationships at subsequent levels in the hierarchy. This structure makes it easy for everyone to understand who reports to whom and the functional areas that employees belong to.

Chapter 6

1. According to Lewin, an organization must first identify what before it can change?

A. Current state

Response A is correct because Kurt Lewin classified the change process into three stages: the present state, the transition state, and the desired state. To start implementing change, the organization has to identify its current state, what is lacking, and potential approaches for improvement.

2. Intended outcomes of change initiatives are defined as specific, achievable outcomes, such as performance metrics or targets.

A. True

Response A is correct because to achieve the desired change, the organization must identify organizational priorities and determine the business goal to establish measurable and time-bound goals. These goals allow the organization to measure progress toward the desired results.

3. Which of the following is a strategy that WLP professionals can use to convince upper management that a change initiative is needed?

C. Remedy selling

Response C is correct because remedy selling defines the process and explains the solution. It is the process of explaining how the gaps between the company's current state and its desired state will be closed, in what order they will be closed, and by whom. In this process, the change manager presents the need for change in a persuasive and convincing way.

4. Which of the following is *not* a primary component to consider when planning for change?

B. Conducting individual training needs assessments

Response B is correct because conducting individual training needs assessments only looks at an individual level and planning for organizational change requires a broader perspective, whereas conducting individual training needs assessments may be a subcomponent of an organizational change.

5. When analyzing the needs of stakeholders during an organizational change process, it is important not to allow individuals who specialize in specific areas of the organization to drive the process.

A. True

Response A is correct because facilitating organizational change is dynamic and complex; it is important that the efforts of specialists are coordinated through individuals who understand the big picture.

6. A training program has been developed to help employees prepare for a new organizational process. While presenting the new course, a trainer sees that some employees are not engaged and sit quietly while others are challenging the details of the process. What is most likely occurring here?

B. The employees may not be motivated and committed to this change.

Response B is correct because change initiatives often assume that all employees are in the third stage of readiness to commit to change, when they frequently are not. To determine their readiness for change, it is important to assess their readiness before moving into the training phase.

7. The purpose of setting milestones is to provide an opportunity to evaluate progress and to reflect on the learning to celebrate the contribution of the team and peers.

A. True

Response A is correct because achieving milestones is one of the best indicators of progress toward the desired goal. Typical accounting measures only address costs in terms of time and money, whereas a change initiative may be directed toward low morale or poor teamwork. It is difficult to measure progress on these indicators without using milestones.

8. What is the order of the five stages of managing a change process?

A. Initiating, planning, executing, controlling, and closing

Response A is correct because in managing the change process, the vision must be cast and clear goals defined as it is initiated. The second phase, planning, defines the scope and resources and establishes the activities to achieve the goals. Executing is the phase where the plan is put into place, and controlling is the monitoring and adjustment process during the execution phase. Closing celebrates the accomplishments and reviews the processes and outcomes.

9. Which of the following analyses is used to identify driving and restraining forces and helps to overcome resistance and complacency in change initiatives?

A. Forcefield analysis

Response A is correct because forcefield analysis, which was created by Kurt Lewin, recognizes two types of forces: driving and restraining. Driving forces help to implement the change, while restraining forces stand in the way of implementation. Recognizing both enables the practitioner to minimize restraining forces and leverage driving forces to help support implementation.

10. Employees go through stages of readiness before they are ready to make a true commitment to change. Which of the following best describes the second stage of readiness?

D. Employees see a need to change but only engage in contemplation and are willing to think about it but put off making a decision.

Response D is correct because the second stage of readiness for change happens after the initial denial of needing to change. Here individuals recognize that change may be necessary, but they are only prepared to talk about it and not do anything about it.

11. According to Albrecht's change response cycle, when an organizational change is first introduced, which of the following response phases describes employees' initial reaction to the change?

B. Threat

Response B is correct because the first phase in Albrecht's change response cycle is referred to as threat. It is characterized by individuals being afraid to change the status quo because of fear of the unknown or a state worse than the status quo.

12. Which of the following is *not* a phase in Albrecht's change response cycle?

C. Complacency

Response C is correct because complacency is not one of the phases in Albrecht's change response cycle, although it is a resisting force that the change manager needs to deal with. Response A is incorrect because problem is the second phase in the change response cycle; it is characterized by individuals seeing change as a lot of work and problems.

13. During an implementation process, a training director is tasked with developing a program to help employees through the change and provide them the needed information to succeed through development of new skills, new knowledge, and even new attitudes toward the change initiative. What process best describes what the training director is providing?

B. Coaching

Response B is correct because coaching is defined as helping others expand and apply their knowledge, skills, and attitudes within a specific context, such as a specific task, skill, or responsibility.

Chapter 8

1. Six Sigma's goal is to move business product or service attributes within the zone of customer specifications and dramatically shrink process variation—the cause of defects that negatively affect customers. Six Sigma may be an effective technique to use in change initiatives because

A. It provides specific tools and approaches that can be used to reduce defects and improve processes

Response A is correct because Six Sigma is a high-performing, data-driven approach to analyzing and solving root causes of business problems that provides a specific methodology to improve processes.

2. Six Sigma is a high-performance, data-driven approach to analyzing and solving root causes and problems.

A. True

Response A is correct because Six Sigma provides specific tools and approaches, such as process analysis, statistical analysis, lean techniques, and root cause methods, to reduce defects and dramatically improve products to increase customer satisfaction and drive down costs.

3. The training department has been asked to join a group attempting to implement Six Sigma processes into their organization. The implementation team is in the beginning stages of review but is looking for input from the training department. At this stage of implementation, where can the training department have the greatest effect in supporting the Six Sigma initiative?

A. Coaching leaders on how to implement Six Sigma

Response A is correct because a significant amount of intensive training is required for Six Sigma leaders, which means that training departments can have a great effect on the success of the initiative and the transformation of their organization's culture and operating systems.

4. One effective strategy used to introduce change in an organization is to select a single media and style to communicate the change.

B. False

Response B is correct because multiple forms of media and style are most effective in communicating about change in an organization.

5. A WLP professional is preparing a communication plan to distribute a list of critical issues regarding the change strategy to employees. Of the following examples, which is *not* a recognized media venue for communication?

D. An experiential learning activity that involves outdoor physical activities

Response D is correct because providing an experiential learning activity that takes place outdoors is not a good way to communicate about change. It may be useful for other things such as team building, but to ensure that everyone affected by the change has clear, unambiguous information about the change, they need effective means of communication.

6. A change management plan should spell out how employees will be personally involved and compensated to help foster commitment.

B. False

Response B is correct because providing additional compensation is not a way to ensure employees' involvement in the change process. To get employees engaged in the change process, it's important that they understand how they will be personally involved to foster a sense of ownership and commitment.

7. A WLP professional is discussing the importance of involving employees to aid the change process. Which of the following is the best reason for involving employees in change?

A. It helps people to become committed to the change.

Response A is correct because giving employees a sense of how they will be personally involved in change provides them with a sense of ownership of the change and thus increases their engagement.

Chapter 9

1. In the sender-receiver model, which term best describes any mindsets, opinions, or biases that may affect how the communication is received?

C. Filter

Response C is correct because a filter is made up of the mindset, biases, and opinions of both sender and receiver and can distort the message.

2. Which of the following is *not* a barrier to communication?

D. Written communication

Response D is correct because written communication is a communication medium, not a barrier.

3. When communicating change initiatives to others, which of the following is *not* one of the key points that will help ensure all involved understand?

A. Provide information at the outset of change initiative

Response A is correct because giving people notice only when the initiative is about to begin is not a good way to keep people informed; people can get panicked if they are not prepared for the change.

4. A WLP professional is providing a peer assessment on a co-worker in the same role. During the feedback process, the WLP professional receiving the feedback politely asks if it is OK if she multitasks and sends a few email messages. What of the following are potential problems with this strategy? (Choose the option that poses the greatest risk to the communication between the two WLP professionals.)

D. A disruptive setting that is a challenge to both WLP professionals communicating

Response D is correct because working on emails is disruptive and misdirects the receiver's attention away from the communication that is taking place.

5. Voice intelligibility, or understandability, depends on several factors. Which of the factors is best described as expressions that serve no positive communications function, such as "OK," "like," and "you know"?

B. Overuse of stock expressions

Response B is correct because expressions such as "OK," "like," and "you know" have no intrinsic meaning and add no value to the conversation. They are simply filler that should be avoided when communicating messages.

6. Using gestures always enhances communication and relaying of messages.

B. False

Response B is correct because incomplete or inappropriate gestures can be distracting.

7. A WLP professional is facilitating a meeting with key stakeholders. The meeting begins with the facilitator making the following presentation: "Good morning, uh, thanks for coming today. Uh, I am, uh, especially thankful for, uh, your participation in, uh, our discussion today about training methodologies."

The intelligibility issue exhibited in this situation can best be characterized as what type of factor?

B. Vocalized pauses

Response B is correct because vocalized pauses refers to the syllables "uh," "um," and "ah" that a speaker may use when hesitating before moving on to the next point. These can be distracting when used too frequently as in the example and can convey the impression that the speaker doesn't know what he or she is trying to say.

8. One way a change manager can help facilitate change acceptance is by having thorough knowledge of how communication moves through an organization. One technique used to identify this flow and where communication breakdowns occur is called a communication audit.

A. True

Response A is correct because a communication audit is used to learn how communication flows through an organization to identify where communication fails to reach the intended audience.

9. Informal networks can sabotage change efforts.

A. True

Response A is correct because members of some types of informal networks may not trust information that comes to them from outside the network. If the network communicates incorrect information or fails to support a change effort, employees may not buy in to and support the change.

10. All of the following are examples of how a change manager can use an informal network *except* to

C. Dicuss personnel issues of specific individuals

Response C is correct because discussing the personnel issues of a specific individual should not take place within a network, but should be kept confidential.

11. What is "noise" in the communication model described in this chapter?

A. A barrier to communication

Response A is correct because anything that gets in the way of the listener receiving the communication is classified as noise. It may be a psychological bar-rier or obstacle between the sender and the receiver, an accent, or the presence of extraneous physical sounds. The goal in communication theory is to reduce the "noise" as much as possible to ensure the message is effectively communicated.

Chapter 11

1. According to various studies, monetary rewards are the highest motivators in reward systems.

B. False

Response B is correct because although money is important to employees, what tends to motivate them to perform—and to perform at higher levels—is the thoughtful, personal kind of recognition that signifies true appreciation for a job well done.

2. Which of the following is *not* an example of a motivational strategy?

C. Tapping into an employee's trust network

Response C is correct because tapping into an employee's trust network is not a way to motivate him or her. Because a trust network is a type of informal network where sensitive information is shared, getting information from it may make the employee uncomfortable.

3. Partnering is a critical aspect of any change initiative.

A. True

Response A is correct because most change managers do not have authority over the resources and performers that are key to the change effort, which means that they have to form partnerships to achieve the goals of the change effort. To partner effectively, it is important to establish expectations and roles early in the process.

4. During organizational change, employees may need new information or skills. Who created the learning style inventory about learner's orientation to four learning modes: concrete experience, reflective observation, abstract conceptualization, and active experimentation?

C. Kolb

Response C is correct because David Kolb developed the learning style inventory to capture the various ways that people process and organize information.

The inventory addresses learner orientation to four learning modes: concrete experience, reflective observation, abstract conceptualization, and active experimentation.

5. Which of the following learning style orientations is best described as "feeling as opposed to thinking"?

A. Concrete experience

Response A is correct because concrete experience refers to the learning style orientation that emphasizes feeling over thinking; people with this orientation are intuitive and open-minded and do well in the absence of structure.

6. During an organizational change, employees must move from the present state to the desired state. During this process, targets of change must go through a transition state. Which of the following is *not* a characteristic associated with this transition state when an organizational change occurs?

A. Low, often undirected, energy

Response A is correct because energy levels during the transition state, while undirected, are often quite high. Therefore, response A is not one of the characteristics of transition states.

7. When developing a reward system, rewards need to have specific characteristics. Which of the following is *not* one of the characteristics that a reward should include?

B. Rewards should always have a tangible value.

Response B is correct because intangibles, such as recognition, may be the most significant reward for some employees. Different people value different things.

Chapter 12

1. The following are the most common management styles *except*

D. Diplomacy

Response D is correct because diplomacy is not a management style. It is a way for change managers to work with other people to build alliances and gain access to important resources.

2. Which management style is most appropriately defined as employees working with no input from management and the processes are dependent on employees?

A. Anarchy

Response A is correct because anarchy refers to a management style in which managers leave their employees to determine work processes for themselves without providing input and feedback.

3. A training manager calls a meeting to discuss strategies for the next fiscal year. She begins the meeting by setting the tone of the discussion and then asks for feedback around her ideas and any other ideas her team might have. This type of management style is best described as a _____ management style.

A. Democractic

Response A is correct because the example indicates that the manager sets the tone of the discussion and asks for feedback about her ideas from her employees. This indicates that the manager both is in control of the situation, unlike in an anarchic situation, and asks for input from employees, which is unlike a dictatorship.

4. All of the following are types of social styles *except*

D. Emotional

Response D is correct because emotional is not one of the four social styles defined by Harvey A. Robbins.

5. People with this social style are often perfectionists who deal in logic and details and tend to keep feelings to themselves.

B. Analytical

Response B is correct because the analytical style is characterized by a focus on logic and details.

6. A person's social style has a direct effect on his or her ability to learn and change.

A. True

Response A is correct because the same individual characteristics that affect a person's social style affect the way that a person prefers to receive and organize new information. For example, a person who is detail-oriented and logical prefers to receive detailed, accurate information.

7. A WLP professional barks out orders to a fellow teammate and is highly demanding of himself and others. When dealing with this person, one should do all of the following *except*

A. Provide thorough examples

Response A is correct because the example suggests that the WLP professional has the driver social style. Because drivers prefer information to be brief, specific, and to the point, this professional would become impatient when provided with thorough examples. Thorough examples are more appropriate for an analytical person.

8. A WLP professional is characterized by many on her team as someone who is constantly making work fun. She is enthusiastic and engaged but sometimes finds herself bored and disconnected when others go off on tangents on a particular topic. This WLP professional's personal style can best be described as

D. Expressive

Response D is correct because an expressive person tends to look for a good time; is enthusiastic, creative, and intuitive; and has little patience for details.

9. Employing emotionally intelligent people leads to greater resilience in times of change or adversity.

A. True

Response A is correct because emotionally intelligent people know their strengths and weaknesses, desires and fears, and joys and sorrows and use this knowledge to adapt positively to changing circumstances. This ability to adapt is referred to as resiliency.

Appendix C
Index

Note: *f* represents a figure and *t* represents a table.

A

action learning
 commitment in, 56–57
 components of, 48–49
 groups and, 52–54
 in learning organizations, 49–50
 meeting management in, 57–61
 questioning process in, 54–56
 See also Kepner-Tregoe process; Six Sigma
  methodology
activities, facilitation of, 38–40
analysis
 business process analysis, 117
 forcefield analysis, 107, 107*t*
 needs analysis, 120
 network analysis, 139–40
 of stakeholders, 104–5
appreciative inquiry theory
 about, 28–29
 evaluation in, 43
 experiential learning activities (ELAs) in, 36–40
 4-D cycle, 30–34, 31*f*, 32*t*, 33*t*
 questioning techniques in, 34–35
 uses of, 29–30

B

Bloom's taxonomy, 50
body language, 135–36
bureaucratic management structures, 71–72, 72*f*
business process analysis, 117

C

change
 agents of, 108, 154
 chaos and complexity theory and, 14–20
 drivers of, 83–87
 evaluation of, 111
 four Cs of, 21–22
 implementation of, 109
 motivation and, 105, 123
 needs analysis for, 120
 planning for, 102–4
 resistance to, 107, 107*t*, 154–55
 selling, 101–2, 106
 speed of, 83
 states of, 151–52
 workplace learning and performance (WLP)
  professionals and, 90–91
change response cycle, 108
chaos, 21
chaos and complexity theory, 14–20
closed-ended questions, 34–35
coaching, 110–11, 121
collaborative leadership model, 79–80
commitment to action, 56–57
communication
 barriers to, 129–30
 diversity and, 137–38
 evaluation and, 122–23
 guidelines for, 130–31
 importance of, 128
 intercultural communication, 61–62
 method selection for, 131, 137
 receiver's perspective in, 131
 styles of, 132–33
 types of, 121–22, 135–36
communication audits, 138–40
communication theory, 128, 129*f*
competition, 84, 88
complex systems, 14–16
complexity, 17–18, 21, 84
confirmative evaluation, 43
conflicts, 88–89
contingency leadership theory, 78
culture, 61–62, 156

D

diversity
 change and, 86–87
 communication and, 137–38
 groups and, 61–62
 importance of, 158
 inclusion and, 145–46

E

ELAs (experiential learning activities), 36–40
 See also Kolb's learning styles
emotional intelligence, 164–65

employees
    change ownership and, 123
    empowerment of, 153
    loyalty and, 85
evaluation
    in appreciative inquiry theory, 43
    of change, 111
    communication and, 122–23
    at milestones, 105–6
experiential learning activities (ELAs), 36–40
    See also Kolb's learning styles
external hires, 86
eye contact, 136

F

facilitation of activities, 38–40
feedback systems, 110
fishnet, 74–76, 75*f*
flat management models, 72–73, 73*f*
forcefield analysis, 107, 107*t*
formative evaluation, 43
4-D cycle, 30–34, 31*f*, 32*t*, 33*t*

G

gestures, 135–36
globalization, 84
goal alignment, 40
Great Man/Woman theory, 77
group approach, 78
groups, 52–54, 61–62

H

hierarchical organizational structures, 71–72, 72*f*
hiring externally, 86
horizontal management models, 72–73, 73*f*

I

inclusion and diversity, 145–46
industrial leadership models, 76–78
information overload, 84
information theory, 128, 129*f*
integrity and values, 90
intercultural communication, 61–62

J

job satisfaction, 85

K

Kepner-Tregoe process, 51–52, 52*t*
Kolb's learning styles, 156–58, 157*f*

L

leadership, 68–69, 76–78, 81–83
learner motivation, 155–56
learning organizations
    about, 87–90
    action learning in, 49–50
    chaos and complexity theory in, 18
learning styles, 156–58, 157*f*
listening, 129–30, 134–37, 134*t*, 164–65
loyalty, 85

M

management
    leadership vs., 81–82
    of meetings, 57–61
    motivation and, 148
    styles of, 164
Massachusetts General Hospital, 4
matrix management models, 73–74, 74*f*
meetings, 57–61, 121
milestones, 105–6
models
    collaborative leadership model, 79–80
    flat management models, 72–73, 73*f*
    horizontal management models, 72–73, 73*f*
    industrial leadership models, 76–78
    leadership models, 76
    matrix management models, 73–74, 74*f*
    postindustrial leadership models, 78–81
    servant leadership model, 80–81
    transformational leadership model, 79
motivation
    best practices for, 148
    change and, 105
    cultural differences and, 156
    increasing, 155–56
    management and, 148
    performance and, 150–51
    resistance and, 107, 107*t*, 154–55
multicultural groups, 61–62
multidirectional structures, 73–74, 74*f*

N

needs analysis, 120
network analysis, 139–40
nonverbal behaviors, 135–36

O

open systems theory, 5–6
open-ended questions, 34–35
organization development, 21–22
organizational realignment, 40, 84
organizational structures, 70–76, 71*f*, 72*f*, 73*f*, 74*f*, 75*f*
organizations
   change drivers in, 83–87
   characteristics of, 14–16
   complexity in, 17–18
   current state of, 100
outcomes, 100–101

P

performance recognition, 150–51
personal mastery, 87–88, 90
postindustrial leadership models, 78–81
powerbases, 140
process mapping, 117–18
process thinking, 117–18
project management, 102–4

Q

questioning and reflection process, 54–56
questioning techniques, 30–35, 31*f*, 32*t*, 33*t*

R

realignment, 40, 84
reflection and questioning process, 54–56
resistance, 107, 107*t*, 154–55
retention and turnover, 85, 152
rewards, 148–50, 152–54

S

satisfaction, 85
servant leadership model, 80–81
Six Sigma methodology, 50–51, 120–21
solutions, 35, 41–43
spoken communication, 134–35
stakeholders, 104–5
summative evaluation, 43

systems thinking, 2–7, 5*f*, 18
systems view, 6–7

T

team building, 89
Theory X, 77
Theory Y, 79
training, 85
Trait theory, 78
transformational leadership model, 79
transition planning, 102
turnover, 85, 152

V

values and integrity, 90
verbal communication, 134–35
voice, 132–33

W

workplace learning and performance (WLP)
   professionals, 90–91
written communication, 134–37

**ASTD Learning System
Editorial Staff**

Director: Anthony Allen
Manager: Larry Fox
Editors: Tora Estep, Ashley McDonald
Editorial Assistant: Stephanie Castellano

Contributing Editors

April Michelle Davis, Stephanie Sussan

Proofreader

Kris Patenaude

Graphic Designer

Kathleen Schaner

Indexer

April Michelle Davis

Thomson NETg Staff

Solutions Manager: Robyn Rickenbach
Director: John Pydyn

Contributing Writers

Lynn Lewis, Dawn Rader

Editors

Lisa Lord, Kim Lindros, Karen Day

ASTD (American Society for Training & Development) is the world's largest association dedicated to workplace learning and performance professionals. ASTD's 70,000 members and associates come from more than 100 countries and thousands of organizations— multinational corporations, medium-sized and small businesses, government, academia, consulting firms, and product and service suppliers.

ASTD marks its beginning in 1944 when the organization held its first annual conference. In recent years, ASTD has widened the industry's focus to connect learning and performance to measurable results and is a sought-after voice on critical public policy issues.

Thomson NETg, formerly backed by the Thomson Corporation, was a global enterprise comprised of a vast array of world-renowned publishing and information assets in the areas of academics, business and government, financial services, science and healthcare, and the law. NETg was acquired by SkillSoft in 2007.